A Beautiful Tragedy

Retta Timmons

ISBN-13: 978-1-7324254-2-2 (paperback), 978-1-7324254-3-9 (e-book)

Table of Contents

About the Author

Contact Retta

Dedication

First and foremost, to God. Wow, it's been a challenge, but You never gave up on me and I am so grateful. Thank You for being patient with me throughout this process. I was disobedient for quite some time due to fear and disbelief, but You loved on me and never lost faith in me. You are truly my strength and there is no greater love than Yours.

Sexual abuse is not an easy thing to overcome—brokenness, hurt, pain, promiscuity, psychological issues and symptoms that become addictions. This book is for every person who has suffered, conquered, or is still dealing with the effects of sexual abuse.

IT'S NOT YOUR FAULT!

Acknowledgements

To my gorgeous daughter Ceané, who has stood by me since day one; our relationship has been strenuous and not of great quality for some time, but we loved each other through it. Without you, I would not have made it this far. You had rough times, but you continued to make me proud of you. You made me smile and helped me to heal through your love. I pray that God blesses you with the desires of your heart and that every life you touch is blessed beyond measure. Always remember to love yourself first and do not let anyone take advantage of you but care for you and respect you. You are truly a survivor and my bright-eyed miracle.

Anna Lee Timmons, my late mother and best friend. Though you are no longer with me, I hope your 'Monkey' is making you proud. There was so much that went on which you knew nothing about. You were right; I was sexually active, but not for the reasons you believed. I was molested — just like you. Thank you for all the lessons, your love, your amazing food, good times and laughs. I wasn't the easiest child to raise, but you did the best you could with what you had and knew how to do. I know you can't read this, but I apologize for the hell I put you through. You are truly missed, and your grandchildren have no idea how amazing you were.

Geneva Conyers, my second mother. You have stood by me, allowed me to share with you, and you still comfort me to this day. I love you so much for who you are. You always shoot straight from the hip. You help me to see things from different perspectives and did not judge me when I informed you of what happened. You are a gift and I appreciate everything you did for Ceané, my parents, and me.

Bishop James David Nelson Jr., Sir, I don't know where to begin other than, thank you. Thank you for being the father I never had. There is so much spiritual wisdom in you and it is time for the world to know who you are. You never gave up on me, no matter how disobedient I was. You loved me from a distance, but I knew you genuinely cared. Thank you for being obedient and following what God told you to do. If you had been disobedient, I may still be out in the world providing sexual favors to any and everybody I could. You are a wonderful husband, father, pastor, and leader. Thank you for starting Destiny Christian Church and for not giving up. The world truly needs to witness what God speaks through you. I know I did, and it saved my life.

Foreword

Everyone is born with destiny, and everyone has purpose. The design of the enemy is to infect individuals at their most vulnerable time, which also happens to be their most impressionable time: the innocence of youth. Seeds of abuse, rejection, perversion and the like— if deposited as a youth—can blossom into unhealthy self-worth, habits, and mindsets as adults. It takes a special person to endure such things and not let them consume your life. *Beautiful Tragedy* is the story of how Retta pushed through and past tragic experiences to become the woman she is today. I have the privilege to pastor Retta. My wife and I have been blessed to speak into her life and play a part in her transformation and recovery. Retta is living proof of what God, determination, and the right circle can produce. Using transparency, Retta endeavors to expose the tactics and spirits assigned to trap, imprison, impede, and distort destiny. While everyone has a story, she has chosen to document hers to help others get through theirs. Retta will take you on a journey from tragedy to triumph and then give you hints of wisdom to motivate you to navigate your own journey. I am proud to continue to watch her journey as she rides to become all she was destined to be. Remember, perspective can influence how you see what life brings. While tragic because of what happens, it's beautiful because of the results that come from it. Retta is able to help women across the world due to her own experiences. Learn from Retta! Don't let your experiences embitter you or shortchange your ability to live. Change your perspective, and you too can call whatever nasty experience a beautiful tragedy. Enjoy!

James Nelson

Pastor
Destiny Christian Church

Pick Up The Broken Pieces

S exually assaulted, rejected at an early age, I was left trying to find out who I was. With each victimization, a new coping skill came along. Whether it was more sex or alcohol, it took everything from me. I no longer felt protected by my parents or loved ones.

I cried out for help. The only ones who heard me wanted to take advantage of my brokenness. They touched me inappropriately or forced me to do things that a child should never even know about. Inwardly, I cried, "Help me." I just want to be loved. Was that asking for too much?

Whether good or bad, I craved attention due to the lack of nurturing my father did not provide, nor did he teach me how a man was supposed to treat a woman. He did not tell me how special, creative and intelligent I was. Never did he validate me or instill my identity so that I knew who I was or how to love myself. He left me to the wolves as if I was a piece of fresh meat waiting to be devoured. Our bodies are sacred, but I was never told that because I literally laid with everyone that wanted to lay with me. Sexual addiction, rejection and low self-esteem took me into deep, dark places I never knew existed.

But, with all the pain and the suffering, I still survived. God came to me and brought an army with Him to help me pick up the pieces. Now, I know my worth. Even my relationship with my dad is healed.

I love Retta. So, love on yourself until you don't need to hear it from anyone. If no one pours into you, pour into yourself. Establish your identity and become the greatest *you* that you can dream of. Don't turn back; run forward. You are loved. You are necessary. You are valuable. You are beautiful. Pick up your broken pieces and use them to become whole so you can help others heal.

The Truth of it All

"For I reckon that the sufferings of this present time are not worthy to be compared with the glory which shall be revealed in us."

(Romans 8:18, King James Version)

Many years of tears, disobedience to God, a life of sin, fear, and everything else I can think of kept me from starting my journey toward wholeness. I was walking through life the way I wanted to—living a façade of happiness. All the while, I was honestly dying on the inside. I had no clue who I was or why I existed.

I was not seeking truth for my life, nor did I care to. All I knew was that my innocence had been taken away from me, and I was unsure how to deal with it. I wanted to be liked — even loved — by everyone. It wasn't until I began to get an idea of who I was that I could leave the needy spirit behind.

Remember that little girl or young lady you called 'fast' because she was dressed scantily clad with lots of makeup on? Remember how you frowned at her, condemned her, or insulted her? That was me.

No one ever took the opportunity to ask if there was anything wrong with me. They did not consider the possibility I was damaged due to sexual assault, rejection or domestic violence? We often comment on the behavior of a person without knowing the reasoning behind their behavior. Did you take the time to speak with her regarding your perspective? My guess would be ninety-five percent of you have responded with, "No."

It's likely you haven't considered how a young woman could lose her moral compass. You may already have it set in your mind that she is just a *hotbutt*. But, we must learn to consider things we see with compassion rather than judgment. That girl may be a broken soul who is in deep pain. She may have become addicted to drugs, alcohol, or sex. If you are too busy judging them, instead of praying for them or just starting a conversation with them, you'll completely miss it.

I was encouraged in my mid-twenties to write a book, but I did not believe I could. At that time, I was clueless as to what prophets and prophecy were. So, I heard the recommendation to write my experiences but dismissed it. *Me, write a book for what? I have nothing to say. Who would believe me and why? What would anyone gain from listening to me? This can't be a way of life. Anyone else gone through this? Nothing I share can benefit anyone else.*

A few months later, I was told the same thing by a different person. They encouraged me to write down my story and share it with others. Once again, I ignored it. My disobedience showed my lack of relationship with God. It was a habit for me. Get up, get dressed, and go to church, because that is what you are supposed to do. I had been doing it since I was a little girl. I was religious, but I did not have a relationship with God. I wasn't really hearing what was being said there. I was missing the life-changing word God was trying to send me through others.

It was not until 2011, when I was reminded by Bishop James Nelson about the task destined for me. I knew that God had to be speaking to me because I had told no one at my church about my past. All of the prophecies I had received had come to me before joining Destiny Christian Church (DCC). All I could do was cry as the prophet told me to tell my story and not to leave anything out. Once again, God was telling me how important it was to Him for me to complete it. Still, I lacked confidence in who I was. How was I to do what God was asking when I didn't believe in my own value and worth, as well as believing in God?

Although I did not know who I was, I was determined to do what God had commissioned me to do. So, I purchased a notebook and began to write. This book should have been completed long ago. But, if it had, it would have been prematurely released and would not have allowed me to complete the healing process. I would have still been broken, unclean, and lost. I would still be ambivalent to who God is. I would still be searching to find out who I am.

Unhappy with life and bitter with my circumstances and myself, I was in no rush to complete this book. I had not given this assignment serious thought, nor did I comprehend how crucial it was regarding the lives of others. As I write this, it helps me to fully understand that during this process, I was maturing.

As I began to speak about what happened to me, people opened up about the traumas they faced. I slowly began to see the importance of this book and the power of sharing my story. I wanted to help people. At the same time, however, I continued to wallow in misery. I feared that telling my story would only make life worse for me. I was not prepared to be called a whore, a slut, or a THOT (that hoe over there) as people heard about the ungodly things I had done with my body.

I faced many demons such as rejection, self-hate, sexual perversion, insecurity, pride, and abandonment, as well as various types of abuse, jail visits, and struggles to survive. Abusers threaten and harm us in so many ways. One of their favorite and most effective tactics is to say, "You better not say anything," or "They won't believe you."

I wonder what would have happened had I disclosed what happened to me. Would the family secret of my abuse be revealed? Would others in my family—such as my mom—share their stories? Too often, many hidden family secrets lie beneath the surface. But people rarely talk about these traumatic ordeals.

Why is it that adult men and women prey on babies? They do not dress inappropriately or behave in a suggestive manner. So, what attracts them to a toddler or any young person? So many of us—children, boys, and girls—who are molested or raped by relatives never tell. Why don't we speak up? Why don't we run to our parents and tell them what took place? Why do we continue to allow the perpetrator to violate us? Why do we shut down and continue to accept this? I can't speak for others, but I grew to realize I encountered this tragedy to assist me in growing strong so that I could help others who survived.

While composing this book, I observed the lack of closeness I have with family and the lack of friends in my life. Was God preparing me for the isolation that would inevitably come with the release of this book? Maybe God knew there would be non-believers and naysayers, but God and I both know the truth of what happened.

Generational curses once plagued my family, not anymore. It stops here! Molestation, oppression, poverty, lack, lust, perversion, witchcraft, and a whole host of other spirits were connected to my family. Fear, along with the other spirits, and not being aware of who I am kept me from getting this book completed seven years ago. That is all in the past. Here we are in the seventh year—the year of completion.

God works everything out for our good. The story of the pain and long-suffering I had to live through may help you to continue to push through and realize that IT IS NOT YOUR FAULT!

Chapter 1

In The Beginning, There Was Hurt

Family is the one thing that we hope to depend on. Family was created to love you, protect you, fight for you, provide for you and make sure that you are walking the right path. Sadly, it doesn't always turn out that way. In our lives as children, we are carefree, loving, and want to enjoy all that life brings us from moment to moment. Unfortunately, we don't realize there is something called 'Generational Curses.' I'm sure many of you have heard of the term 'Generational Wealth" or maybe not. I'm wondering how many of you are looking up those terms right now?

As I share with you what I endured, consider the curses that may have been upon your family's life or are still there because no one slayed those Goliaths off the family bloodline. When you hear the term "Generational wealth," it's the opposite of a curse, which is blessings of the many generations in your family. If no one breaks the curse(s), you may never see the blessings or the wealth.

As I look back over my life, never in a million years, even if you paid me, would I believe that I, Oretta Caleetha Timmons, would be a published author; twice, a published model, a college graduate, or even seen on televisions or movie screens across the globe. Due to the trials I endured in my youth, my mindset did not allow me to believe that I could have or deserve greater. Even now, as I reflect, it brings me much joy. However, back then, it was just something to do for attention. I could not appreciate it because I did not appreciate nor love myself.

As I grow, I now understand the depths of gifts and talents I have and that they must be used for good. I understand why many, even strangers, talk to me regarding their life, due to God providing me with a compassionate heart that leads me to be a great listener as well as being able to provide wisdom to the broken. After a few months of missing high school, I'm now the first in my family to graduate college. For multiple semesters I held a 3.5 GPA, in college, after many years of believing I wasn't intelligent. I befriended many in my courses due to me being very nurturing. I participated in programs that led to me sharing my gift to inspire others at speaking events.

Although I'm retired from modeling and acting, my face can still be seen on television shows and movies such as 'The Wire,' 'House of Cards, ' and others. I've successfully matriculated from thinking in lack to thinking I'm great in the earth. Not only have I published my own memoir, but I'm a coauthor in other published works. After 11 years of feeling like a failure and female staff trying to terminate me at my job, I've been promoted to another position with a pay increase. You can't tell me that the God I serve is not good. You can't tell me that God does not take care of His children, because He does. Please remember, "What the enemy meant for evil, God meant for good."

It wasn't always easy to have faith and believe, but when you surrender to God and allow Him to heal you, all things are possible. You see, things weren't always great in my life, although they looked that way and much of what I faced, kept me in limited beliefs about what I could achieve. Now, I know I can "Do all things through Christ Jesus who strengthens me." It wasn't always easy to celebrate myself and if you keep reading, you will understand why. Are you ready?

It's tough facing abandonment or thinking you're being rejected. It would be hard for any child whose parents left without any clear answer about when (or if) they would ever return. It's difficult to live with the threat that you may never be embraced by your parents again.

*July 5, 1971, *****

I, Oretta Caleetha Timmons, named after my paternal grandmother Oretta and my Aunt Louise, was born to Johnnie and the late Anna Lee Timmons. I was born in Baltimore City, but eventually moved to Manning, South Carolina, when I was three months old temporarily and returned to South Carolina at the age of three years old and remained until I was six years old.

The reason for the move was that my mother worked two full-time jobs until she became ill. Working two full-time jobs did not leave much room to care for my brother and I. It wasn't that she did not love us, but desired to have us properly cared for, due to not having a support system. My father was a street pharmacist (a drug dealer), who was also a partaker of the product. He was not available mentally or emotionally, and sometimes physically to care for us.

They would visit us in South Carolina quite frequently. Food, clothing, and toys were always packed to capacity in the car for my brother and me. I loved seeing that Brown Convertible Mustang or the Lincoln coming up the dirt road, but I hated to see it leave. They never stayed for long, but I will always remember crying as they headed towards the highway, leaving the dust of the road behind them. I believe this is where the spirits of abandonment and rejection were embedded. When you're left to feel as if you're not wanted, that leaves an open door for the enemy to attack.

I don't have clear memories of our day-to-day living in South Carolina other than spending a lot of time at my great-grandparent's home. I also remember visiting my cousin Shell's house and playing with Bozo and Cow, who also lived down the road. Four years later, my two-month-old brother, Leon, came to live with us at my Aunt Giselle's and Uncle Gavin's home. They were my second set of parents. My Aunt Giselle was a great cook and a loving woman. Aunty kept an immaculate home. Everything was always in place. My Uncle Gavin, on the other hand, was a drunk. His breakfast of champions, corn liquor. He would get up, take a drink, and head down to Ms. Jane Water's bar to play pool and drink some more. He frequented a second bar that was not far from the house. I was placed at the bar or played with Keisha, Ms. Jane's daughter. My brother, though, was invited to play with the men.

Aunt Giselle made sure we were clean and fed; she cooked multiple times a day. I would constantly hear, "Bo-Cat, Bo-Cat," which is the name my uncle called my aunt. I don't know the exact age I was when my Uncle Gavin began inappropriately touching me, but I was very young. No more than four years old. I suppressed my painful childhood memories because they were excruciating. Not only was I molested, but also called ugly and told I would only be good for laying on my back. Those were hurtful words and for a long time, I believed them.

I loved to play outside and it was mostly done at my great-grandparents. Their home was the gathering place for the family, so at any time, the house would swell from two people to twenty. Grant and Coral Coates, my great-grandparents, were the absolute best. They had a small farm with chickens and hogs, which I helped to feed. My great-grandmother was no joke in the kitchen. I especially loved her Pearlo rice and Lemon Meringue pies, but everything she cooked was delectable. She was of a medium-build and part Cherokee Indian, which is why I believe her skin was so soft and beautiful. She also had long, beautiful, silver hair that she let me brush and plait, only to later cover it up with a wig. Granddaddy was a bald, fluffy gentleman of medium height with the same lovely complexion and skin as grandma.

Grandma Teal was the one who taught me how to kill, skin, and cut chicken. Most of my time was spent playing outside, alone, mostly and helping my great-grandma cook and clean. My grandfather raised hogs and chickens. He also collected and sold junk. They had a thriving vegetable garden where I enjoyed picking watermelons, along with other fruits and vegetables. I remember sitting on the front porch after picking and snapping peas along with other vegetables for my grandmother to preserve in mason jars or prepare for dinner on very hot summer days. The enjoyment of the day came when my grandfather would leave to go junking or to the slaughterhouse.

When my grandfather left, we took the opportunity to raid his dresser drawer that was consistently packed with a variety of snacks: Circus Peanuts, Ginger Snaps, Raisin Crème Pies, Nutty Bars, Star Crunch, Maple Nut Goodies, and so many other yummy goodies. Yes, I was a fat girl from the very beginning. We were smart enough to wait for the dust behind his truck to clear before we attacked the drawer. We knew that *he* knew what we were up to. But, he never complained.

My favorite days were Sundays. Like clockwork, I would wake up, take a bath, and get dressed before sitting down to a plentiful breakfast. Our Sunday buffet—made from scratch and cooked with plenty of love—included biscuits, sausage, grits, pancakes, eggs, toast, ham, and lots of other goodies. I enjoyed my biscuits with thick King Syrup or Roddenbery's Cane Patch Syrup. Cane patch syrup was thick and it added a touch of heaven to anything it landed on, including biscuits, eggs, and bacon. While we were eating breakfast, dinner was being prepared. Love, lard, and grandma's heart were the first ingredients in every recipe. That is what made everything so good. Cakes and pies—oh my! My grandmother was a fantastic cook and taught my mother how to cook. From the Coconut cake to delicious Lemon Meringue pie that could win any competition, I loved it all. My mouth waters just thinking about it.

Our family attended Zion Baptist Church. It was a small church but full of love, morals, values, God, and great food. My grandparents were deeply involved in church. Granddad was a deacon, and grandma was a Sunday school teacher for over thirty-five years. Although the church was very loving, it was one place you did not play around in. One Sunday, I think I had ants in my pants; I could not sit still. Toe-tapping, hand-clapping music was never in short supply. I was moving around a lot. Grandma told me to sit down and I did not listen because before I knew it, a shoe was coming toward my head, from the choir loft. I never misbehaved in church again.

With grandma teaching Sunday School, I knew what every young person should know about the Bible at that time. I knew the Ten Commandments, 23rd Psalm, and other scriptures. I was so young when I was introduced to God, that I did not take it seriously. The stories I learned were just that—stories. I had no idea how to connect or to reason how it was supposed to affect my life. I attended church because I was told to. But I didn't fully understand who this invisible man was that people were singing about and praying to. Was He another fairy tale character?

Once service was over, we would either eat dinner at church or go home and have a humongous feast. The highlight of the evening was going to the family room and back porch, where grandma would play the piano and sing a multitude of songs. Those moments were precious to me. It was family time.

My grandmother often shared about her life. One of my favorite stories is why she left school before finishing. She stopped going to school in the third grade because her shoes were worn, which caused embarrassment.

Like clockwork, she would sit at the piano, tell the story and then began to sing. My favorite song was, "Everybody Ought to Praise His Name." It spoke of how we should praise God and give thanks because the birds do it; why shouldn't we. She was well-rounded and honored God with her life. Upon returning to Maryland, we would only see her during the summer, which is when we returned to South Carolina or when a relative died or celebrated another year they were blessed to be on earth. Between the age of five and six years old, we returned to Maryland.

After returning to Maryland with our parents, we lived in Woodington Garden Apartments. We resided in the first court where there were plenty of kids and many families: the Stewarts, the Fabres, the Sewards, along with so many others. We dwelled in several apartments, but it started in a two-bedroom apartment where my brother and I shared a room and slept on bunk beds. It was always cozy and clean. My mother was very meticulous about our house and the way it looked. She worked hard at keeping our home clean and in order. My mother was the disciplinarian and did not mess around. When you disobeyed Anna, the wrath of God came down. In no way was I a perfect child, but I tried to do my best. I merely wanted to be like the other kids in my complex. To me, they had so much freedom because they could stay outside late and go places I could not.

There is a difference between city and country living. No more dirt roads to play on. There was no more picking fruit and vegetables from the garden and no more robbing granddaddy's snack stash. I would not get to see my cousins as much. But I was happy about no longer being chased with snakes and fish heads. I thought the worst was behind me. I no longer had to slop the hogs or be touched inappropriately. I thought the sickest part of my life had come to an end. I did not know the worst of it was ahead of me. Upon returning to Maryland, I attended Irvington Elementary School. The school was very nice, filled with kids and I liked it a lot. The weekdays were like clockwork; we got up, dressed, had breakfast and were dropped off at the bakery every morning. The bakery was definitely a daily highlight. Another highlight was meeting friends that I am still friends with today. I met Natori Wallace, Tracy Blake and Moneen Brady, along with a ton of others. During this time, we prayed and said the 'Pledge of Allegiance in school. Teachers also had the authority to punish you by tapping your knuckles with a ruler. Due to the pain it caused, it only took one time for you to get hit, so you never caused another problem in class.

During the summer months, the school held camp where I met many new children if we did not return to South Carolina. We enjoyed box lunches which were very tasty. I remember always receiving extra fruit, juicy nectarines, to be exact, due to some kids not liking them or an extra lunch was there for the taking. Camp was Monday thru Friday and always fun. This is where I first learned of some of my talents. I was introduced to dance and Double Dutch jump rope, along with many other activities. We played games, ran free, and ate snacks. I was such a tomboy growing up.

I was also very girly and received the best of everything. Since my parents were financially stable, I had many toys and clothes. I remember my parents would shop for us at Korvette's twice a year, to purchase our clothes. They would purchase our wardrobe for Spring and Summer and then again for Fall and Winter. My parent's owned multiple vehicles. We were all snazzy dressers and would eat out once or twice a week. We were kind of like the Jefferson's, but not as wealthy.

My brother and I were extremely close and were always together. We played hard until the streetlights came on. Once they did, it ensured we were in the range of our mother's voice through the window. If she called, you better be near that window to respond.

Our family unit was close, and we spent a lot of time together. My mom made us home-cooked meals daily, breakfast included. Everyone loved her cooking, because she was a replica of grandma when it came to food. Just like my great-grandmother, my mother could make anything from scratch. Friday and Saturday was pretty much the only day we might have something someone else cooked.

On Fridays, we ate carry-out unless my mother prepared fish, cornbread, and salad, which was a staple meal. Sometimes, we would go to Farrell's ice cream parlor. Mommy deserved a break because she stayed busy all day. My mother kept an immaculate home and welcomed everyone. The neighborhood loved to visit our home.

My mom would do anything for anyone. She was very loving and giving of herself. In the summertime, she would open a snack shop to provide treats to the neighborhood kids. They loved "Ms. Anna," and many of them called her their second mom. I remember a time when a neighbor passed away. Guess who collected money on her behalf?

Those were just the types of things she did. The phone rang quite often, for advice because she was so intelligent. If she did not have an answer, she found the solution. To be honest, my family missed out on many lucrative ideas due to a lack of trust on my father's behalf. Both of my parents were offered opportunities to build businesses, which would have brought about wealth and a major change for my family. An opportunity my father passed up is still in business today and I wonder if, just if, that restaurant or catering business was built for my mother, would she still be alive. I don't know if his being reserved was due to something that happened in his childhood or later in his life.

Although they were great together and loved each other, there was also a dark side. My parents physically fought one another. I never knew why they fought, but it was done on more than one occasion that my brother and I witnessed with deep fear. This was another area that led me to believe violence or pain meant love. I did not know any better. It also shaped some of my future relationships. I guess every couple has their good and bad days, but it should never lead to fighting. Outside of the fighting, there was lots of love and fun to be had.

Summertime was spent at camp, here in Maryland or we returned to South Carolina and stayed with my Aunt Gizelle or my great grandparents for the summer. As we grew older, amusement parks or the beach became regular trips. The beach was a family outing on a much larger scale, with lots of food and other family members. Summers in South Carolina became a little different due to my aunt and uncle being separated because we were staying at another relative's house. At this time, we attended "Feed A Child" camp in Summerton. We would walk there and return to my cousin's house afterward. I was introduced to something a little different at his house and I'm not sure why I was chosen.

Laurence and Caitlin did not live that far from the camp. Upon reaching their home, we all played outside, but Laurence would ask me to come into the house. I don't know what he said to the other kids, but they never came inside the house. He would tell me where to stand as he began to touch himself. I stood there, not knowing what to expect or what to do. At this age in my life, I did not realize this was something that pleasured people. It seemed to be something excruciating due to the noise and faces he made. After several minutes, a white substance would cover the walls like silly string and the noises he made became almost like a scream. I would jump back in hopes of it not getting on me. Once he finished and relaxed for a minute, he would laugh and tell me to go back outside and play, which I did. A word was never spoken as to what took place in that room, until now.

It happened a few times, the summer ended, and we returned back to Baltimore. As I grew older, the summer stays became less frequent in South Carolina. I was spending time with my family and, as I grew older, with Natori and her family. My maternal grandmother lived in the 500 block of North Monroe Street. We went there almost daily and sat on the steps, eating snowballs or ice cream and playing with the neighborhood kids. My mother's father, Lee, died of cancer when we were young. He allowed me the run of the house when it was just him and me. My grandmother told me that she returned to the house one day to find everything in the kitchen covered in flour, including my grandfather and I. He was sitting in the chair laughing. Of course, my grandmother was not happy that she had to clean it up. My grandmother was a thin, dark-skinned lady who could also cook. She enjoyed watching baseball when it was in season, but the family favorite was the World Wrestling Entertainment (WWE).

We all loved watching and attending live wrestling matches as well. We did not miss a live event unless it was too costly, like WrestleMania. We would sit on the steps together for hours, and we had so much fun. I would assist my grandmother with cleaning her white marble steps and cutting the grass in her small backyard on the weekends. Not only did she sweep the sidewalk and gutter in front of her home, but also the sidewalk and gutter of the homes on each side of her home.

I did not have a problem with helping because I knew homemade cake, ice cream, wrestling, and snowballs were soon to follow my chores. I'm sure you can tell by now, great food has always been a staple in my life. My uncle Bud and his family: Aunt Willona, Tasha, Naomi, Sam and Tito, our cousins, lived at the end of the block.

There was always something to do because there were kids throughout the neighborhood. Life was good, and my memories of those terrible things that happened were long gone. It seemed that I was living a different experience now. I think what I loved most was hanging out with my Aunt Linda. She was the coolest aunt ever. She spent a lot of time with me. I loved to hear her sing. We would often sing together and tease each other about who sang the best. It was just good fun.

A time came when my family began to struggle financially. It was some of the worst times of my life. It was embarrassing, but there was nothing I could do about it. On several different occasions, my father was incarcerated, causing our standard of living to decrease, due to the loss of his income. We did not dress as nicely. We could no longer afford nice shoes and had to buy cheaper footwear from the grocery store sometimes.

There came a time we lived on public assistance. We no longer had transportation and we either traveled by mass transit or walking. I remember being embarrassed at having to go to the store with a food stamp coupon book. Kids would tease me because, in those days, having food stamps meant you were poor. I also remember receiving blocks of cheese provided by the government. At least, I think it was cheese; it didn't melt well!

During these times of hardship, my brother, mom, and I walked from Irvington to Monroe Street carrying bags of laundry. It was an hour-long walk, but my mom did what was necessary to make sure we were okay.

I wondered why my mom did not work to help our financial situation. Then, one day I saw red lesions all over her body. Her belly swelled as if she was pregnant. She later passed away and I never had the opportunity to ask about her health. I learned—after she passed away—that she suffered from Bi-Polar Disorder and may have had asbestos poisoning.

It wasn't until much later that I learned that my mom had been raped by my Uncle Nathan at a young age and that my great-grandfather had fondled her as well. Molestation and rape seems to have been a generational curse on my family. In knowing that, I wonder how many other relatives have suffered at the hands of family members and nothing was ever said or done about it.

The trauma in my life was suppressed so much so that it took a funeral to bring back the memories of what happened. In her early hundreds, my great-grandmother passed away. In the Black community, when one passes away, it's called a 'Family Reunion' due to that being a time you get to meet and/or see family that you did not know existed. During this time of grief is when it all came back, as I, along with my daughter and nephew, journeyed to South Carolina for her funeral. It was about a 7-hour drive, due to bathroom breaks and having to break up mini meltdowns and meal time for the children.

It was great to return to South Carolina after so many years had gone by. Our first stop was to see our cousin Marcus, the son of Gizelle and Gavin, but he was not home. By chance, I ran into my Uncle Gavin outside of his trailer, which was down the road. I stopped to talk with him and see how he was doing. We talked for a while. He offered to let us stay with him, but I was not comfortable with that. He then called me 'Bo-Cat' and tried to kiss me. It was not an attempt at an innocent kiss, as from a father to a daughter or an uncle to his niece. It was an attempt at a kiss like two lovers would. That triggered what took place many years ago. I felt violated. It was the same feeling I had when he fondled me as a child. I knew I needed to go as he continued coming on to me. I could only imagine what he would have tried to do if I had stayed in his home. Not just to me but possibly the kids because they were so much younger.

I quickly put the kids in the car, and drove to the motel to check-in. I was mad, hurt, protective, and proud all at the same time. I was proud at that very moment that I did not allow what had happened to me to happen to those babies in my care. After processing what happened, we walked into the motel room, freshened up and began our rounds of family visits. Our second stop was my Aunt Fannie's house. While visiting, our cousin Lydia stopped by. It was great to see everyone, but that recent encounter with my uncle stayed with me.

His role in my abuse took place in those stages of drunkenness, and I was quite young. There were nights he would come into my room and touch me inappropriately. It happened a few times throughout my stay but eventually stopped. A feeling of hate began to come over me and it made me sick to my stomach. I did my best to keep it from ruining my time there. I continued smiling through the rage I was feeling. I managed to keep it under control and enjoy my family during this time of our great loss. My babies were able to meet some of their family members, although they were really young. We returned to Baltimore and life kept moving.

I don't know what it was about me, but I was always fighting. While I did not start them, I certainly finished them.

I have a small frame, so I was bullied a lot. I don't know if people thought I would allow them to say what they wanted to me or mistreat me. Perhaps my height made me a target. Perhaps people assumed I would not fight back; eventually, I did. This was a learned behavior as I watched my parents argue and fight on many occasions. My brother and I frantically watched one night as my mother was swinging like a rag doll from the back of my father's truck. We cried and screamed until she returned. There were other times, but I'm sure these are the events that led to my rage.

I remember blacking out whenever I would fight. That caused many black eyes and busted noses- never mine. I don't say that to brag, but to show you that when you have so much pain and anger built up inside you, you don't know your own strength. When I was no longer timid and fearful and began to fight back, I was more respected. Big, tall, short or small, I made sure I provided the necessary pain so they would never give thought to wanting to fight me again.

Desi, a kid who was taller than me and twice my size, would kick me on the way to school nearly every day. One day, I refused to deal with it anymore, and I commenced to whipping her tail. Not only was Desi surprised, but others were too. I never had to worry about Desi again, and my mom made sure of that. My mom went to speak with Desi's mom. She knocked on the door and made it clear, "You want to fight, pick with someone your own size." My momma was feisty. I guess that is where I got it from.

Questions

Here are some questions to answer as you process through the sexual abuse you suffered.

Have you admitted that you were abused? Yes / No

Have you acknowledged your trauma? Yes / No

Have you accepted your trauma? Yes / No

Have you announced your trauma? Yes / No

What trauma have you faced? How does it make you feel?

_____

_____

_____

Did you ever desire to tell someone but were too afraid? Why?

_____

_____

_____

Have you faced other traumatic experiences? If so, what was it? How did you handle it?

_____

_____

_____

_____

With the trauma that took place in your life, have you acknowledged and accepted it? How do you know? Why or why not?

_____

_____

_____

On a scale of 1-10, 1 being not at all and 10 being completely, how much of what happened do you blame on yourself? And why?

1-2-3-4-5-6-7-8-9-10

You Got This!

Thank you for not giving up on yourself! I know it wasn't easy to relive your past pain. But look at what you've accomplished. By answering these questions, you've taken the first step toward speaking up, speaking out and putting your hurt and pain behind you. You may even help another abused and broken person to share their story and begin healing. Do you know that you're a hero? I admire you for being so brave. Keep sharing because you are saving lives, whether you know it or not.

Chapter 2

The Beginning of Destruction: Next Level Impurity

E arlier, I spoke about the fondling, but this is where the real damage was done. I think we all could somewhat agree that our grandparent's home allows us freedom to have fun we aren't allowed to have at home, and the sheer joy of all the candy and snacks we desire. With that being said, weekends with my grandmother and aunt were priceless. Being away from my mother, who I thought was mean, was refreshing. I was attending middle school at the time. However, I was clueless as to what I was about to endure in my young life.

At the time, my aunt was dating Aurelio. He was a tall, somewhat thin, light complected man, with pretty hair and use to wear these shorter than short shorts and socks that had color rings around the top like the Harlem Globetrotters. They were together for quite some time.

Aurelio was at my grandmother's almost daily. His character did not display the monster that was hidden inside. He seemed like a gentle, caring person, whom I never thought would hurt me in any way. One night he was there a little later than usual. I was a kid and thought nothing of it. He told me when everyone else went to bed and I came into the house to come to the basement. This was not something he had ever asked me to do, until now. I was always taught to respect my elders, so when the neighborhood kids went in, so did I. I was clueless as to what was about to take place. It did not happen every time he was there, but too often. He first started at my grandmother's house in the basement until my aunt moved up the street. Aurelio introduced me to vaginal and oral sex. Anal sex was attempted, but he was too big.

I went into the basement where Aurelio was. He began by making me feel his penis while inside his pants and then he would pull them down. I felt horrible and knew this was not right, but what could I do? I was too afraid. He taught me how to French kiss, which is something he enjoyed. While he had me rubbing him, he would rub on my vagina before inserting multiple fingers. It hurt so bad that he would cover my mouth to keep anyone from hearing me scream and cry. Later he would shush me. He even taught me how to take it without screaming anymore. I still cried. I was told I better not tell because no one would believe me.

He later taught me how to please him orally without using my teeth. He said, "Males don't like you using your teeth because it doesn't feel good." He liked oral sex a lot as he always made me do it before penetration. He would tell me what to do and how to do it so that it was euphoric for him. "Move your mouth up and down." "Suck it when you go up and down." "Come up and take it out of your mouth and put it back in." He also liked me to suck the head of his penis harder. My jaws were always sore.

During penetration, I would often bleed until my body adjusted to it. It makes me sick to my stomach as I sit and write this. But this was my life—my routine. It was the same all the time. Why didn't anyone come looking for me? Why couldn't the silent screams be heard from the basement? I can't begin to tell you the numbness I felt. There seemed to be no hope or security for me. I hated and loved life all at the same time. I loved life because I finally thought there was freedom at my grandmother's, but what I thought was freedom became bondage of a different type. There was no relief. I desired love and affection but not that which would cost me my identity and my purity.

Later, my aunt moved several blocks up the street from where my grandmother lived. One day out of the blue, my aunt asked if Aurelio had bothered me. With my head held down, I said no. I knew my aunt loved him, I did not want to get into trouble, and I did not want to hurt her. I loved being with her, but not her boyfriend. I was so glad when my aunt stopped seeing him because the rape stopped, and Aurelio married another woman. Had she sensed what was taking place? Did she have an idea? Had she seen or heard something? I felt so helpless and we blame ourselves for the action(s) of these sexual monsters. If only a strong foundation and love was materialized from the beginning, things would have been much different. Communication with your children is so important, although it may be uncomfortable. Talk to your children about appropriate and inappropriate touch. Talk to them about sex. Don't make them hug people, family or not, if they are uncomfortable.

Conversations of that magnitude never surfaced in my home, at any time. If they had, I would have felt comfortable enough to share what happened no matter what threats I received. It infuriated my family, especially my mom, because she truly loved her family and did not play about her baby sister. My mother established a personal invitation to his wedding, along with my aunt, grandmother, my cousin, and myself. We entered the ceremony, bold and uninvited. The biggest, baddest of them all, my mom, big bad Anna, took Latasha, the daughter of Aurelio and my aunt Linda, a baby at the time, into the church to show Aurelio's wife. She also gave Aurelio a piece of her mind before we exited the nuptials. Seeing this made me wish that I would have shared with my aunt what he did to me. Maybe, just maybe, she would have left him sooner. It was believed that he had contracted A.I.D.S/HIV and passed it on to her. My aunt later caught pneumonia and passed away. That was one of the saddest times of my life. My favorite aunt was gone forever, and that rapist was still alive and free.

The dynamics of my family changed when my younger cousins were sent to live with their paternal grandparents. My aunt and Aurelio were the parents of two girls and a set of twin boys. When my aunt passed away, my mother wanted custody of her nieces because the twins were already at Aurelio's parent's home. She wanted them so much so that she began to make strides by getting a larger apartment, as well as furniture for the girls. Needless to say, with all the effort and preparation by my mom, the children were taken to their paternal grandparents with the boys. The reason for this happening was because my grandmother would not sign the necessary papers for them to stay with my mom.

My grandmother thought that she would be left to take care of the children, but my mother was not that kind of woman. That placed a deeper wedge in the relationship between my mom and grandmother. The girls later ended up in foster homes, and I am unsure what happened with the boys. I would go see them until Ms. Renita—their grandmother—no longer allowed me to. I saw Aurelio years later, and he claimed that he missed Tim and I but acted as if nothing ever happened. What happened to my family? What happened to all the days of running up and down the street, eating snowballs and ice cream, watching wrestling and just being together?

I was scared as I grew older because I was not a teenager when he began molesting me; I was a child. When I came of age and was able to get tested, I did so on a regular basis because I saw the results of this horrible, untreatable disease. My physician thought I was crazy for taking tests the way I did. The results always came back negative, but I continued to get tested because I was sure to educate myself about this deadly disease. I was terrified that I would die young, but God covered me in His blood. I wasn't glad my aunt had passed away because she was my favorite and I loved her so much, but I was glad Aurelio never came around again. And I was thankful I had not been exposed to AIDS/HIV.

The fear of rejection, abandonment and the molestation opened me up to a world of promiscuity and sexual perversion. I felt unloved for so many reasons. Although my father was in the home, he was not the father that guided or loved on us. He took care of us financially, but the emotional, mental, physical love a father gives to his child(ren) was missing.

The molestation and rape had taken my purity away from me, so I was receptive to any male who gave me attention. Rejection is not a spirit to be played with. It will have you running from pillow to post with anyone, doing anything. My entanglement with males went into the double digits, which at the time included ménage-a-trois', orgies, lesbianism, performing stripteases at parties, and sleeping with the groom-to-be. This destructive behavior, of course, led me to contract many diseases at various stages in my life.

When you hide something like molestation and rape, and you are not healed from it, it makes you think that you are already an adult, even when you are not. Molestation and rape are more than physical acts. They are spiritual acts. They take pieces of your soul. It causes deeper damage than most realize. I did not even know the full names of most of the people I engaged sexually with. I remember my mom asking me the full name and address of someone that I had contracted Chlamydia from, and I could not provide her with information. Chlamydia and Gonorrhea were the diseases I contracted on a regular basis. No one ever taught me how precious I was and that I needed to protect myself from all the diseases that I could contract. My mother never inquired as to whether anything happened or why I was living so negligent.

Believe it or not, this began in middle school. Was this something everyone went through? Was I the only one? I couldn't ask anyone because shame and guilt was on me heavy. How could I ask without someone thinking I was dirty and 'too grown' for my age? I couldn't bear what my friends would think of me. I continued to excel in education and then came graduation. A damaged mess on the inside but the persona of a champion being displayed on the outside. It was time for high school. Due to my impeccable grades, I was accepted into some of the best high schools in the city. Western and City were high on my list, but not my mothers.

Like others, my mother assumed that I was 'fast' and she needed to keep tight reigns on me. I presume that is why my mother did not want me traveling too far from home to attend school. In my mind, the school up the street was garbage. It took the wind and the drive for greatness from me. I no longer strived for honor roll status. I did well for the first two years and I even enjoyed being a part of the ROTC program.

I excelled in the program and rose to the occasion every opportunity I was given. I was promoted to a Sergeant and eventually was the leader of our drill team. We were invited to showcase drills and there I was, 5'0" but I had the attitude of someone that was 6'6". My voice bellowed commands in a powerful manner and the team followed with great execution. Although ROTC was teaching me discipline, I was not willing to follow through with it at home. I wanted more freedom, not knowing what it would really cost me.

Due to the altercation between my mother and I, I later moved out. I was beyond scared of her and did not want to follow the staunch rules she laid out. I spoke with my friend Dacia, who in turn talked with her dad and I moved in with them. Her family consisted of her father Harold, her brother Howard, Dacia and I. Sometimes Mr. Harold's girlfriend Brenda was there as well. My life wasn't exciting because I pretty much went to school and returned home.

Dacia and I were good friends, but I spent a lot of time alone except when I was with Howard and his friends. That consisted of motorcycle riding, bowling, dining out and just 'good ole fun.' Mr. Harold was gracious enough to provide me with shelter and food. Although it didn't feel like home, I had a place to lay my head and rest. It wasn't always an easy or peaceful rest because, unbeknownst to everyone, he was also molesting me. Unlike many of the other times molestation took place, he did not threaten me. He would enter the room where I slept and began to rub himself, rub on me and then began to rub his penis against me. This was not something I asked for, but I do believe, due to my earlier abuse, this is what I owed him since I lived there. I no longer saw rape and molestation as a violation but as a natural part of my life. Abuse will cause you to look at life differently. It provides perspectives that cause negative emotions and disheartening outcomes in life. You don't think clearly about what the outcome of a situation will be due to your desire of wanting to be loved, accepted and liked. If I told or asked Mr. Harold to stop, would he put me out? I later moved in with another family because Dacia's mother desired me to leave. It didn't happen immediately, but I did.

Questions

If you were abused mentally, physically or emotionally, take a minute and think about things that you did that made you feel dirty and ashamed. Answer the following questions.

What symptoms have you acquired due to abuse? (i.e., rejection, increased sex drive, alcoholism)

_____

_____

_____

_____

Have you been able to figure out the root of the problem? If so, how are you coping with it?

_____

_____

_____

_____

Do you remember those that hurt you? Have you forgiven them? Have you forgiven yourself? If not, draft a list of those that hurt you in any way.

Once you have completed that list, draft a letter of forgiveness to them and then one to yourself. In the letters, release all the hurt and pain that you are feeling. Allow yourself to write every emotion that you have gone through, every bad thing that you have wanted to say or do to them and yourself. After drafting the letter, you have the option to send it or not. Whether you do or not, you must forgive them and yourself.

You Got This!

Wow, you're a fighter! You've been through a lot. You've been abused, contemplated suicide, and feel alone. I've been there, but look at us now. You are still in your right mind. No matter what you are facing, you are still fighting to achieve the greatness within you. Don't give up and certainly don't allow anyone to stop you. You got this! Stay focused, keep dreaming and watch how far you go.

Chapter 3

Damaged Goods – Lust, Perversion and Rejection, Takes Over

This chapter will give you an idea of what lust, perversion and rejection can do to you. When your purity is taken away, it opens doors in your life that take you places you would never imagine going. Most don't understand the spiritual aspect of what happens. The doors opened in my life, all dealt with promiscuity and fornication—oral, anal, and vaginal sex, menage-trois', orgies, men, and women. I allowed people to do whatever they wanted to me and quite frankly, some of it I enjoyed. It was fleshly pleasure that was causing me spiritual pain and death.

God created sex to procreate between a husband and wife as well as binding them together as one. Mark 10:8 reads, "And the two shall become one flesh; so then they are no longer two, but one flesh." In layman's terms, this means that every person you have sex with you are now married to, in the spirit. Your body not only exchanges fluids, but your souls are now intertwined. Everything God creates which is good and perfect the enemy perverts. I was literally a garbage dump. Now that I look back over my life, I can pinpoint where every issue I face came into play.

No one knew the challenges I faced throughout life. I was dressing it up, putting makeup on over it, and acting out in various ways to deal. My classmates thought I was stuck up, mean, and many other things. Those feelings that arose due to rejection, abandonment, bitterness, perversion, shame, hurt, and self-hate were significant in my life and played a considerable role in my behavior. I had very few friends: male and female. I did interact more with the males than the females because they provided solace. We were able to converse on a different level, and I did not understand women and their dislike towards me.

The inquisitiveness inside of you is considering every relationship that you have ever been in at this moment, right? You're thinking about what caused you to become entangled with those you honestly had no interest in. You went from relationship to relationship and bed to bed because you wanted to be loved. You craved attention that seemed genuine, but the desire was nothing more than lust and perversion taking over. It was never love but sexual desires. Reflect on the relationships you have been in as well as the behavior you've displayed. When you really understand the spiritual aspect of what happened when you were abused, it's easier to understand your actions. In all of it, you are not your decisions and deserve to be healed and made whole.

I share some details of relationships, sexual by the way, that I participated in. In some of the relationships listed, I allowed sex to take place because I thought I owed them something. I surely did not believe I had the right to say no or stop. I did not have a clue what it was to receive things from someone and not owe them anything. I was involved with many men, whom some are still internationally known entertainers, producers, and authors today. Rejection, lust and perversion don't care how you get what you desire, as long as you get it. It started with my uncle and grandfather molesting me, but it was the rape that caused more damage.

Molestation and rape steals your confidence, your identity and hope for anything great. Rejection is a spirit that wants you to believe that no one loves you or wants to be around you. Rejection makes you do things as healed you would never contemplate. I am talking about that relationship that is so toxic; if you don't get out of it, you will end up in the hospital or dead. Yeah, that relationship. You have rejection issues that keep you in that relationship. Rejection tells you, "You're ugly and no one else will want you." Rejection tells you, " Your hard work does not matter." It's a lie that we hold on to tightly because we don't know who we are. It steals our identity, which causes us to accept anything we are told as truth. It seems that rejection began with me when my parents dropped me off in South Carolina. I never knew if they would be coming back or not.

My rejection continued on throughout my life, but it really reared its very ugly head in middle school or at least recognizing it a little more. Constantly fighting and filled with rage. I did my best to get along with others. There were some I got along well with and others not so much. Home was not the greatest and school was definitely not a place of refuge. High school was not any better. The fighting continued. However, I became more promiscuous due to the rape. I did not date much then due to not being 'the popular girl' in high school. The boys I liked did not want me, and the ones that wanted me I had no interest in. The ones that were interested only wanted to have sex with me, and some did. After becoming broken, some of us tend to believe that having sex with them makes them want to stay. That is a lie!!! There was one with whom I shared interest with. He was always so sweet and so kind. His voice was as sweet as a lullaby. He could sing you into a peaceful place. He was kind and a genuinely warm spirit. He was a gentleman, a very anointed and gifted singer, as well as being able to make you laugh. At this time, I began to realize that I had very few female friends but many male associates. I guess you could say I had plenty of associates, not real friends.

Hanging out with Lamont and listening to him sing was always a joy for me. It took my mind off the pain I was fighting through. Not everyone had the privilege to meet my parents, but Lamont did. Even now, I still have a vivid memory of Lamont sitting at the dining room table looking nervous. He frequently made appearances at my house because we enjoyed one another's company. We weren't together for a long time, but I enjoyed the time we spent together. Lamont could sing anything, but to hear him sing "A House is Not a Home" by Luther Vandross would send everyone into a tizzy. He always found a way to keep me smiling, and that was wonderful. What I enjoyed about Lamont as well was that he never made any sexual advances towards me. It all came to an end a little while before he passed away. When Lamont passed away, it hurt me to my heart. The joy of song, his friendship, and laughter was taken away through death. I had no one to turn to, and that was painful for me.

Denise, a classmate of mine, told others that I acted like a complete fool at the funeral by crying loudly. Neither Denise nor the class knew my relationship with Lamont. Nonetheless, I will never forget that relationship and what he meant to me.

He was one of the few that created a bond with me while others disliked and wanted to fight me. My relationships or lack thereof caused many physical altercations. At this stage in my life, I'm still fighting. Even today, I am not sure as to why I fought so much. In the unawareness of my authentic self and lack of self-esteem, I had no idea how to process the things I was dealing with. I never liked fighting because of what it represented at home, but I had to defend myself. The scary part was blacking out during fights, which did not allow me to know my own strength or control how violent I could be. It was not a pretty ending for any of my opponents though.

Was it my "smart mouth" or did people think I could not fight, which drew me into combat? Perhaps they thought I was afraid of them. I never provoked a fight, though. People underestimated me due to my petite stature. But my reputation soon spread. After a few occurrences, that all stopped. There were many times I should've said no or stop. Whether it was someone, I met on the street or those that I already knew, if I was groomed correctly, there would have been a lot of no's and stop.

"No," in my loudest voice should have been stated to Coach John, Dacia's dad and Mr. Parks. I was quite uncomfortable in each of these situations. With Dacia's dad, I didn't say no because I thought I might not have a place to live. I felt that I owed him something since I was not working and he was providing food and shelter. He was an authority figure and I was still a kid, who never strayed away from what I was taught. "Stay in a child's place." "Do what an adult tells you to do." Now, I must admit, this was not my first encounter. It undoubtedly was not one I was expecting, nor did I welcome it. But it led me to feel that if someone did something for me, I owed them.

I hear your question as to whether it was molestation or not; I did the same thing. Yes, I questioned it, but I also realized that I did not consent. It happened a few times before it stopped, and I was thankful for that. Now, her brother, on the other hand, was different. I did not say no but provided a nonverbal consent. I was hanging out with him, and he was very charming, funny, animated, intelligent and popular. The weekends were when I spent most of my time with him.

Riding motorcycles, bowling, horseback riding, go-kart racing and so many other things Howard allowed me to do with him and his friends. Every weekend was a new adventure. Then one day, it happened. Howard and I were the only two in the house. That day, we ended up having sex just like I did with the previous males before him. It was another sexual encounter that had no meaning, nor did I have a reason or excuse as to why I did it. By this time, it was just a natural thing for me. Mr. Harold and Ms. Verna were divorced, but Ms. Verna was the one to take me to my parents and suggested that I return home. The conversation did not matter. I did not return home and began looking for somewhere else to go.

The incident with Mr. Parks occurred when I moved in with Carlita. Micha, whom I was friends with in school, introduced us. Carlita had a large family. Everyone was kind and treated me like family. They were the creators of "Steeldreams." It was a marching band, which Carlita eventually talked me into joining.

Things were okay, and I was doing well in school. It was my senior year, and I was determined to enjoy it. I was the captain of the "Pom-pom" Squad. I sang in the choir, ran track, participated in the talent show and co-created the charm club. It was a fun time, although I missed my family. It was phenomenal to entertain thousands of people while marching in the parades for both bands and traveling. It took me back to the fun times when I use to ride in the parades.

At this time, I was dating Kevin, who was also a Steeldreams member. Kevin was dark-skinned and not that attractive, but he was kind to me. He worked and had a car, but he lived with his parents. We would spend time at his house, attend rehearsals, or he would be at Carlita's home. The one thing that I struggled with was Kevin having horrible breath. I kept gum and mints on hand, but he needed them.

It was an okay relationship. Looking back, I would not have done it again if given a second chance. We stayed busy due to Kevin managing a group called "Total Kaos." This group included some talented young dancers. The group consisted of Bryce, Gordon, Damon, Jamey, Dionte, and Larry, who was the last to join. Due to my relationship with Kevin, who managed the group, I was able to meet many celebrities, which was really cool.

Kevin and I had disagreements like any other couple would have, but our last encounter was due to me missing school on picture day. I dressed in my pom-pom uniform and waited for Kevin to pick me up. I thought he was going to drop me off at school, but we ended up at the Baltimore City Health clinic because I transmitted an STD to Kevin. I pleaded with him to take me to school to complete my pictures and then go to the clinic. But he would not do so. I was furious and needless to say, that was the end of our relationship. I thought I was happy, but honestly, I was not. I went through a stint of depression. It wasn't due to our relationship ending, but due to suppressing my abuse. I didn't understand how rejection worked or because I was even affected by it, I let anyone in.

My life was in complete turmoil. So much so, that at one point and time, I stopped attending school. I missed two or more months of my senior year. I returned to school after some time having to fight physically and mentally, trying to succeed and graduate. I remember going to my math teacher because math was the one class that would keep me from graduating. He put up a fight, but I did what was necessary to graduate. I completed extra assignments and put forth just a little more effort so I could walk across that stage.

In my senior year of high school, I was sleeping with Coach John, who taught physical education. I have a feeling I was not the only one, but I feel it is necessary to share. It started out innocently, as they all do. He asked me to take a ride with him one day, not knowing it would be to his home. He parked, and we went into his house.

At this time, I was old enough to understand what was going on physically, but not mentally and emotionally. It was the touching of my breast which started the offense and abuse. He would have sex with me as I just laid there like I was dead and allowed him to do whatever. It occurred almost on a weekly basis. After I graduated, we continued to keep in touch, but not on a sexual level. I even attended events with him and a few other coaches the following year. In my mind, this became the norm for me. It became okay, but it was not. The continuous unwarranted sex with men did not help me in establishing the necessary father figure I desired and needed. When you are abused, there is a scent you carry, which abusers have a keen sense for. I was mentally, emotionally and spiritually ill, all without knowing at the time.

Eventually, I worked multiple jobs so I could purchase things that I needed to survive, as well as some things I wanted. No one in my family accomplished the feat of graduating high school, and it was about time the tables turned. Remember, my parents did well financially without a high school diploma, so I could only imagine what my life would be like with one. I returned to school, not doing my absolute best, but I managed to graduate in June 1989. I did not care because I did it. That is all my father ever asked of me. Up until high school, I was an honor roll student.

Even in the excitement of prom and graduation, I wondered when would the older men, who I considered to be mentors or held a position as a grandfather, due to them being older, would stop being the abusers. I did not know the Parks that well, but it was later that Mr. Parks decided he wanted to know me better. I was tired and had no comprehension of what was on me. Was there a sign on my forehead or was there an inviting facial expression that told them to do what they did to me? One day, Mr. Parks arrived at the house, and I was there alone, which I was quite often. He came in, and we hugged as usual. We exchanged small talk as we usually did, but Mr. Parks had a different agenda this day. Like many others, he took another piece of my soul. He began by fondling me, which led to him trying to penetrate, but he could not gain an erection.

We both heard a door, and he quickly pulled himself together and departed my room. It was Katina coming home, and she never knew what had taken place before her arrival. Thank God, that was the first and last time he ever touched me. Through the years, silence and fear built up. I began taking up for myself but not the way I truly needed to. I began working at Sachs Stride Rite and Lerner's so that I could have some income to get the things I needed. Senior Prom was coming up, and I was about to become an independent adult. Prom night came, and I was somewhat prepared.

My mother had already purchased my gown, and I needed to purchase my shoes and figure the rest of it out. Finally, I was able to purchase my shoes and the other necessities. Although I knew I would be attending the prom, I did not know who I would be attending the prom with. It ended up being Deandre Dobbs, who previously dated my friend Natori. Neither of us had dates, nor were we in relationships. I wasn't the bell of the ball, but I was there. Of course, I was made fun of by fellow classmates upon entering the prom. I thought I looked pretty and that was all that mattered.

Although sad, I did my best to enjoy the evening. I wanted to be complimented and adored like the popular girls in school, but it never happened. What would it take for me to be liked? Would I ever be liked by anyone other than males? Graduation time came, and high school was over. My life was not mapped out, and nor did it sound like many of my classmates. For the most part, they knew what they desired to do and what they wanted to be. However, I had no desire to become great, or to be honest, to become. As I began to venture out into the world and began working, I became more interested in the opposite sex. Thomas was a handsome older man that Marsha was dating. Thomas informed Marsha of his single son, 'Carlos.'

Carlos and I talked on the phone and had provoking conversation. It was time for us to meet. Thomas brought Carlos over to the house one day, and we both smiled as big as we could. He was a light-skinned young man with curly locks. He was short, but I did not care because he was very handsome and funny.

One day, he finally asked me to come over. Carlos lived in Honsing Ridge with his mother and grandmother. Mr. Thomas and Marsha had a bet going as to whether or not Carlos would get the goods. Well, Marsha lost. She did not know my history or the actual state of mind I was in.

I arrived at Carlos' and met his mother and grandmother, who were very kind to me. He came downstairs, we both smiled and greeted one another. His grandmother used her detective card as she really loved her grandson. Carlos grabbed my hand and led me upstairs. We talked and listened to music before heading to bed. Yes, we had sex that night. He was very gentle, and I enjoyed being with him. When you are dealing with rejection on top of abuse, as well as other spiritual issues, the outcome(s) are endless due to your skewed perspective of everything.

Carlos was a great kisser and very handsome to boot. He and I became an item, so I thought. I got to know his family. We did not spend every day together, but his grandmother and I spoke daily. She really took a liking to me. I used to think his mother, Ms. Veda, did not like me, but she was a very firm person. His grandmother used to tell me pretty much everything. Carlos and I never partook in any extra-curricular activities, but I did not care.

We saw each other a few times a week. Other than paying for my transportation or feeding me, he never gave me money. I would never receive anything from him because he said I was always dressed nice, and my hair and nails were always done. Carlos, just like my father, was a street pharmacist. He kept thousands of dollars in a shoe box, which he had plenty of shoes...and money.

I guess I could say that I was a family favorite, not knowing that there were other women in Carlos' life. His grandmother told me once that Carlos had a book with the names of the girls that he was seeing and what he liked about them. She said next to my name it stated that I was beautiful, intelligent, loving, kind and lots of fun. Carlos and I were together for close to a year before he left for the Navy. He did not want to continue with a long-distance relationship as he thought it would be unfair to me that he would be away. We wrote to each other and exchanged pictures, and we would see each other when he came home on holiday. I was still in contact with his family and saw his grandmother on a regular basis.

By this time, I had acquired my first car, a 1989 silver Infiniti M30 coupe with mirror tint on the windows. This car was beautiful and provided me the opportunity to spend more time with Carlos' grandmother. I took her wherever she needed to go. I loved her so much, and it was not just because she kept me informed on what Carlos was doing, but she genuinely cared for me. It was not what I knew a relationship to be. Upon Carlos returning home, he later became incarcerated and that definitely created an end to our relationship. He didn't believe it was fair to me and I was tired of taking the bus to Hagerstown to visit every weekend.

My next relationship began with Marcel Black, who is a Caucasian male. Marcel dated black females all his life, but this was a new experience for me. I was open to it because I always liked being exposed to different things. You cannot give me a chicken box and expect me to be overjoyed. I was a young woman who demanded great food and being exposed to new things. Yeah, I hear you, but I always have liked trying new things. It does not make me a bad person or bougie; I want more than what the corner store has to offer.

Marcel had the prettiest eyes that would change color and the cutest smile. Marcel and I met at Woodlawn bowling alley in the early nineties. We talked about three months before we began dating. There was a large group of us that would go bowling every Friday and Saturday night. He approached me and continuously teased me, which showed that he had an interest in me. After bowling, most of us went to breakfast, and he began sitting next to me and taking care of my portion of the bill. He was sweet, and I enjoyed spending time with him.

One thing led to another, and we began to hang out on our own. We would take long rides on his motorcycle, and he allowed me to drive his car. At this time, his vehicle was my mode of transportation. We spent a lot of time together, and I enjoyed it. We enjoyed going to the movies, go-kart racing, batting cages, dining out and a host of other activities. We truly enjoyed being together, and there literally was never a dull moment. Marcel introduced me to some new things, and I loved it. He was such a gentleman, and that was refreshing,

He would open doors for me, pulled out my chair, ordered my food, surprise me with gifts, and check up on me to make sure that I was okay. The first gift I ever received from Marcel was a beautiful cashmere sweater. I needed to pay my Hecht Company bill, and he offered to take me. I walked by a crème and gray Cashmere sweater. I made a statement about the cardigan and proceeded to pay my bill. The next week he showed up with a very pretty, gold gift box wrapped in a big, red bow. When I opened the beautiful box, it was the sweater. I hugged him and thanked him.

He introduced me to Godiva Chocolates, Rhebs Chocolates, and some other things and I introduced him to Jesus. I ended up moving in or, more so, staying with him at his mother's house for a brief stint. Ms. Jennifer did not like me, but Marcel cared about me deeply. His mom was cordial, but she really did not want Marcel dating me or any other black female. After staying with his mom a while, we got our own place. He allowed me to select the furniture and he purchased it. I always wanted his input, because it was ours. We were making our apartment a home.

We practically did everything together. We went grocery shopping together, hanging out and just enjoying each other's company. We began attending church together, and he even joined the choir. Life seemed to be so great with him. He would send or bring me flowers weekly, along with candy sometimes. I can see him walking through the door with those beautiful blue eyes and that huge smile. It always made my day. I would come home to nice gifts, which was a change of pace for me and I truly appreciated it.

We were at the bowling alley every Friday night with associates and then breakfast in the morning. We would head home, get some rest and prepare for Saturday's activities. We would go grocery shopping and run errands to make sure the house was well stocked. We communicated about everything. Marcel was very clean and respectable. The only thing I did not like was seeing his hair in the bathroom sink, but that is a pet peeve in general. I know, I know, there was something about it that irritated me though. I'm sure there was something about me that annoyed him.

Marcel and I became serious, so I felt it was time for him to meet my parents. We took the short trip to my parent's home since they lived nearby. I knocked on the door, and my mom answered and let us in. I introduced Marcel to my parents. My father was not at all impressed because he did not care for Caucasian people, so that was hard for him to digest. Mommy, on the other hand, was happy just because I was happy. Mom, being who she was, offered Marcel something to drink. They conversed for a while before we headed out to enjoy the remainder of the day.

One of the roughest moments is when we disagreed. The disagreements had to do with other males at times, but it wasn't what Marcel assumed it to be. Our first disagreement looked strange with this petite black woman chasing after this Caucasian man and they were both yelling, and he was crying. We ended up on Frederick Road, where I was trying to talk some sense into him, but the more I said, the more aggravated he became. I began to see a side of Marcel that I did not know existed. I'm unsure if there was some trauma he faced as a child or built-up aggression or anger. I only saw the sweet side of him.

So much so that he began cutting his neck and wrist with a butter knife he took from the house. I called 911, and he ended up being admitted to the hospital psych ward. After a few days and being placed on anti-depressants, he returned home. It was not much longer before we ended up moving into his mother's house. Marcel was independent but also a momma's boy. I was not sure of where our relationship would go from there, but I stuck in there.

The sick part of this relationship is that Marcel became abusive. I was shoved into walls and pushed down stairs. I stayed in this environment because it was what I grew up in, and I thought it was love. I saw my parents physically fight one another. In between us loving each other and fighting, we ended up getting engaged twice. The first proposal I don't remember, but I did select my own ring. The second proposal was beautiful. We invited our friends to join us at Harrison's Pier Five Restaurant. I was naïve and just thought it was a dinner with friends.

I thought nothing of it, and the waiter uncovered it to reveal a box, which contained an engagement ring. I began to cry as I was not expecting this. Marcel removed the ring and asked if I would marry him. I responded with a yes, but no one could understand me through the crying. I finally stopped crying and restated my response so that everyone could hear.

Marcel and I made many great memories, and I could only imagine what others may have occurred if we had remained together and did it the right way. We returned home, and things were beautiful for a while. Marcel helped me to build my credit by becoming a co-signer for credit cards. I did not get out of hand with them, but I was not that knowledgeable regarding credit cards or credit reports.

I began making wedding plans by purchasing a wedding planner and shopping for my wedding gown. After searching for weeks, I finally found the one that I believed was perfect for me. We talked about the wedding and trying to set a budget. We had a part of the wedding planned out. It was going to be a beautiful ceremony. With planning in progress, things once again fell off track.

We begin spending less time together, and the relationship started to deteriorate. I began to spend more time with friends and less time with Marcel. He allowed me to continue to drive his car and it got to the point that I did not care anymore. We eventually moved back in with his mother.

After a few months, we were at it again, which pushed us to the end. This particular night, we were arguing before

Marcel threw my clothes on the front lawn and pushed me down the steps. By the way, there were five steps I missed on the way down before landing on the grass. A neighbor heard us and called the police. The next day I temporarily moved back home. I established a friendship with a young lady named Andrea who I bowled with. She was a single parent.

I established a friendship with a young lady named Andrea, who I bowled with. She was a single parent. We both wanted our own place, but our income was not enough to do it alone, so we became roommates. We searched for apartments until we found something that we both liked, which was Hamlet West Apartments. It was a two-bedroom apartment with a living room, dining room, kitchen, and balcony.

We did pretty good for a while, and we had a falling out. She moved out, and I had the apartment to myself. Marcel and I were going back and forth in and out of the relationship. There were times he would just show up at the apartment without calling or anything. I would never let him in because my rule of thumb was to never just show up without calling first. He would yell out my name and cause a scene. This was unacceptable and the ending of our relationship. My lease was ending soon, so I began to search for another apartment. I returned to Woodington Gardens in another court, which is where we moved from.

Once again, Marcel and I tried to rekindle our relationship. We would spend some time together but nothing like before.. Needless to say, we did not make it to six months. I had

Marcel's car and received a call from him to come to Howard County General Hospital. He was very calm when we spoke. I arrived only to find out that once again, he attempted to commit suicide. This time it was by cutting his wrist. His mother was there with him. He asked her if she could step out into the hallway so we could talk. We spoke briefly before he asked for his car keys and we began to argue. At this time, he also grabbed the necklace I was wearing and ripped it off my neck.

I remember cutting my hands trying to hold on to the necklace. Marcel's mother returned to the room and asked me to leave as Marcel and I both shed tears. All I could do was cry, as I exited the hospital. I was nowhere near home and felt even more broken than I ever felt before. I walked back to his car and tried to break the windows, but I could not. I tried to figure out who I could call to come and get me, and at this time, it was my best friend, Chadrick. He picked me up, and we discussed what took place. I arrived home and cleaned up my hands. I did my best to carry on with my life.

I continued to work and live my life. I began working at the Chimes, which provided a place for the developmentally disabled to gain work experience. I was the receptionist there. That position allowed me to meet some friendly people. One of my responsibilities was to sign everyone in and contact the appropriate persons on the executive side.

The Chimes gave me the opportunity to partake in various fundraisers and help in a different way. I loved watching the clients work and having conversations with them. My favorite event was the western fundraiser we had. It entailed great food, an auction and western line dancing. We had to dress in western apparel. That was a great evening. I was dating Marcel while working at The Chimes and later met Trey, my husband, through Mr. Ethan. Mr. Ethan would bring the clients and drop them off at work and later pick them up. We spoke and had wonderful conversations daily. One day he asked about my personal life and my relationship status.

Mr. Ethan always spoke of how nice I was and how I should not be alone. He continuously told me how great of a young lady I was. He told me one day that he knew of a young man that he wanted to introduce me to, his stepson. I gave him my contact information, and I heard from Trey a few days later. Mr. Ethan also brought Trey to my job. At the time, he was home on leave from his naval tour. Trey and I spoke on the phone for a day or so before we met in person.

I went to his mother's house, and we sat in the basement and talked for quite some time. I do believe that we kissed. The next time we saw each other, he picked me up and took me to a carnival and won stuffed animals for me by playing basketball. Trey and I had a great time whenever we were together. It seemed as if we had known each other for years. We spent a lot of time together during those thirty days.

We fell in love - or what we thought was love - in thirty days. Thirty days went by quickly, and it was time for Trey to depart. I knew I was going to miss him, but I had no idea that he impacted Tim's life so much that it would cause him to cry.

Trey left for Bahrain, and we talked almost every day. We both missed one another. My phone bills were over $1500 a few times, which Trey paid for. He was only gone a few months before he asked me to join him.

I began preparing for the journey by getting my passport which caused me to travel to Washington, DC. I needed to have it expedited so that I could travel at the appointed time. I prepared boxes of hair products and clothes to be shipped there. Trey informed me that I could wear what I wanted at home and on the base, but when we went into town, I had to dress modestly. It was an Arabic/Muslim country, and I did not want to be arrested or possibly killed for not following their laws. It did not bother me though. I saw Ms. Kaye, Trey's mother, before I left.

She made me promise her that we would not get married. I promised, but we all know how that ended. I wish at that time I was emotionally healthy, so I would've taken her advice. We were doing adult things but still immature when it came to marriage. It was August when I left for Bahrain. The flight lasted nineteen hours, which allowed me to dine on Arabic food for the first time and it was some kind of good. I raved about that food for a while. I remember arriving in Bahrain, and it was HOT! It was not humid but dry heat. Trey met me at the gate, as Tameme, his landlord, allowed him to use his truck to pick me up. We were very happy to see one another.

We returned to his flat, which was a quaint little place. I was awakened in the morning by prayer, which is played over a loudspeaker. I thought it was one of the most beautiful things that I had ever heard. Trey showed me how to get to the base so I would be able to travel there when he was at work. It was not that far of a walk from where we were staying.

If we did not eat on base, we would go home and cook. We shared the responsibility of cooking. One thing I loved about him is that he did not want me to work, but I still had credit card bills to pay back home. He knew the role of a man and made sure that he provided for our home. After talking to him about how bored I was and just did not want to sit in the house, I went to work.

My first job was at the commissary as a cashier, then the liquor exchange and then the Rec center. I had to keep the place clean, pop popcorn and make sure the youth had a great time. Two young ladies became very attached to me. Cary and Becky were the greatest. We had girl's day where I pampered them with mani/pedi's, and I even did so for their proms. They were with me a lot when Trey and I weren't together. Working in the rec was my favorite job on the base, thanks to the kids. Working in the liquor store allowed me to meet more of the soldiers on the base. They were all kind, friendly and drank a lot. Some of them were daily regulars and some of them I saw once a week.

I had the pleasure of meeting Anderson, who was of Hispanic and African American descent. He was tall, slim, light-skinned and wore glasses. He came in maybe every two weeks, and we talked briefly. After a month or so of him coming into the store, he gave me his number. There was nothing wrong with my marriage and Trey and I were very happy. The relationship between Trey and I developed so quickly; we never got into the particulars of our past that much.

I never informed him about my past and the trauma that I had been through. Two of the symptoms I dealt with from being molested were lust and perversion. They both cause you to feel empty inside. It makes you feel like no matter how much sex you have, it's never enough. Whether it was with Trey multiple times per day or masturbating multiple times a day, it was just never enough. There were times he had to work overnight and not only did I need sex but I wanted it.

I recall the first night Anderson and I got together. We conversed throughout the day, and he called me to let me know where to meet him. It was in a motel not far away from where we lived, so I walked there. I knocked on the door, and he answered. We both smiled and embraced one another with a hug. We chatted for a bit before he began to kiss me on the lips and then on the neck. I loved adventure, albeit unsafe and unwise.

While we kissed, we began to undress. He would kiss and bite me, and I wanted more of it. What made it even more intense is that I had a fetish for certain accents and Anderson was bilingual. He was very attentive and gentle. You would've thought we were in love, but it was lust.

We ended up being together twice, but nothing happened the second time we met. I made a dangerous mistake and invited him to our home one evening due to Trey working an overnight shift. He came over, and we talked for about ten to fifteen minutes. The next thing I know, Trey was turning the key in the door. Surprisingly, we kissed, and I asked what he was doing home.

He first checked the balcony and then all the rooms. I knew that Trey had been informed by Rafeit that a male was at our home. While checking the rooms, Anderson jumped from the balcony. Our doorman, Rafeit, informed Trey of what happened when he left. Anderson and I never saw each other on those terms again, and I ended up finding another job on base. Trey never mentioned it, and we carried on with our marriage as nothing had happened.

Trey and I returned to the states. We went to Maryland first and stayed with his mom until it was time for us to move. I met his family, and they seemed to like me. My parents were ecstatic that I was back on American soil. We had returned just in time to celebrate my twenty-second birthday. Yes, you read it correctly. I was only twenty-two, married and lived through hell. This particular day we traveled to my mom's house, where she had a cake and balloons for me. We stayed for a while and enjoyed conversation and cake with my parents.

Home visits seemed to take place every weekend whether it was the both of us or one of us. Some weekends Trey would go fishing with Dennis, a friend he met on base in Virginia. He really loved fishing. I believe the worst weekend ever was returning home and receiving the news that Carlos had been shot. He was in a comatose state and hooked up to multiple machines. His entire family was at the hospital when I visited.

I walked in, greeted everyone and grabbed Carlos's hand. I began to speak, and he opened his eyes for the first time and smiled when he heard my voice. I stayed as long as I could because Trey was due to be back at work and we had a disagreement because we left later than what was planned. He was not happy with the fact that I wanted to be with Carlos, but he was my friend.

The ride home was very quiet. Trey was not happy about my visiting Carlos or him getting home later than he wished to. It was a little rough for a minute because he believed that I was still in love with Carlos, but I wasn't.

We continued on with life as usual and back to our regular routine. A few months went by, and we did our usual weekend visit home. Trey wanted to stay home this particular weekend, but I had a fashion show. I drove home and performed in the show and visited with family. I returned home on that Sunday to be welcomed by a message from a young lady looking for Trey.

The message said, "Hello, this is Lia, and I really enjoyed spending time with you. I apologize that I could not come and spend the weekend with you in Virginia, but when are you coming back to DC?" I was fuming, despite my infidelity overseas. I waited for Trey's arrival that evening. He finally arrived home, and we greeted one another. We talked about our weekend apart, and I asked him who the young lady on the voicemail was. He claimed he had no idea.

I told him I would understand if she asked for him by nickname as Trey is a common name, but she asked for him using Treyton, his real name. We began to argue. After the situation escalated, I called my mom. This was a major mistake, but I was frustrated. We ended our call, and a few minutes later, police arrived at my door. My mom had called them.

I informed them that everyone was okay and they departed. I called my mom back. That weekend, she and my dad arrived with a U-Haul truck to haul me home. No, I had not given any thought to what I did. Honestly, I had forgotten about it. We, the abused, tend to suppress our memory due to it being painful. I stayed with my parents for a little while before moving in with Kavon, Taniece, and Walter.

Trey and I conversed off and on about possibly getting back together, but years later, it ended in divorce. We never successfully tried to work it out. We did reconnect years later through Facebook. We chatted then began talking on the phone. We conversed for a few months about his children, the issues he and his wife encountered and how his mother purchased a BMW truck to have enough room for her grandchildren.

Our conversations came to a halt after months of conversing. It ended because he would occasionally ask about things that I thought were inappropriate. We laughed and joked about it, but I always said no. Once his marriage was back on the right track, he said, "Do you really think I would take the chance of losing what I have? I have too much to lose." That was the last time we spoke for a while.

I don't like to use sexual assault as an excuse, but you reap what you sow. If you do good, you receive good. If you do harm or hurt someone, it will come back to you. I never wanted to do many of the things I did, but when your soul is broken, you don't know what you may end up doing because you're open to things working in you that you are clueless about.

So as I said before, I was involved with men and women. I was just sex-crazed and did not know how to do without it. You've heard about some of the male encounters, so now let's talk about the females.

My first encounter with a woman began with a co-worker. Rhonda and I were close and we talked about anything. I met her family and became an auntie to her son. We had a relationship outside of work, so we talked a lot.

One day we began to talk about my interest in women. This conversation carried on into the evening and the next day. The discussion continued for a few days before we later had an encounter in the ladies' room. This is where my first experience with a female came into play.

A few days later, we ended up becoming sexually intimate. I did not know what drove me, but I just wanted to please her. All I kept thinking in my head is what felt good to me; I hope it felt good to her. I wanted this more and more. So we met up again.

Guess what, she wasn't enough. Blackplanet and Craigslist became sites that I searched daily because I needed and wanted more. My next interaction with a woman took place between myself and couples. When lust and perversion takes over, your hunger for deeper sexual activity grows. You begin to explore areas that you would have never considered.

With the help of Blackplanet and Craigslist, more men and one other couple followed. I won't go into detail, but know that the last couple I was entangled with lasted for a little over two years. The difference between the first and last couple is that the last couple visited my home, I got to know their children, and it lasted for more than a night, as I stated above. I was a complete mess. Lust and perversion had me tied all the way up and I was not trying to let go. Yes, it felt good for that moment, but little did I know I was killing myself on the inside. My soul was beyond fragmented. I had husbands and wives that I did not walk down the aisle with.

I was enslaved for quite some time. This was around the time I began to really seek God. I needed and wanted change. At the time, it seemed that death was my portion because I was already dead inside with light nowhere in sight. Conviction began to set in, and I needed things to change.

With things weighing so heavy on me, I began to settle down and my appetite began to change. I knew that I was not created to be with women but men. Not multiple men, but one man, God created for me to spend the rest of my life with. I was not well versed in knowing my place as a woman, so I began looking for the one, instead of allowing him to find me.

I loved being on the dance floor. Throughout my young adult years, I was in the club with my friends Wednesday through Sunday nights, along with other activities. There was Club Choices, Hammerjacks, Fantasies, Paradox, Latin Palace, Gatsby's, and O'Dell's, just to name a few. Whether we were all around dancing together or dancing with a male partner, we turned the floor out.

One night I was alone at Choices. I generally wore all black - something short, sexy and fitting. Being on the dance floor allowed me to be in my own world. On this night, as I walked around the club, house and club music were playing, and I went in because they did something to me. Jackson, a friend and security guard, was working this time and a very attractive young man caught my eye. He was about 6' tall, slim and could dance. When I say dance, I mean he belonged on someone's tour as a backup dancer. Little did I know that we would embark on a journey through life together.

I went over to Jackson after coming from the ladies room to ask about the handsome lad. He told me his name was Marvin. He asked if I was interested. I was. Jackson told me he believed that Marvin was single. I did not ask any more questions but went to the stage to dance. One of my favorite songs came on, and I went all in. As I moved around the stage in performance mode, I caught a glimpse of Marvin watching me.

I was not the dancer he was, but I definitely could hold my own. When I got into it, I zoned out without realizing he made his way to the stage. He began to dance with me, and I had not realized it. I kept dancing until the music changed and he leaned down and asked my name. I replied, and we danced for a bit more. When the evening ended, we exchanged numbers and spoke the next day. At this time, he was living at home with his mother, and I was on my own.

Marvin and I were inseparable. We became so close that we would go clubbing together sometimes. But one of my most favorite times to spend with him were on Saturdays. He danced on a show, 'Teen Awareness,' which was hosted by Anita and Dane. It was a talk show for teens that discussed very important issues.

Some days I sat on the bleachers as a guest, and other days I sat in the break room where all the celebrities came through. In that space, I had the pleasure of meeting so many stars, including Maia, who was also a dancer on the show, Tech, of Nasty by Storm, Misha Elonzo when she rocked the matching Russell sweats and a host of others. They were all kind and took a moment to sit and talk with me. Those were fun times for me, and I enjoyed the atmosphere.

Marvin and I became very intimate and cared deeply for one another. He was at my house quite regularly, and then I began to allow him to use my car. I worked at night, and he was looking for a job. I cared about him and wanted to see him succeed. He introduced me to his family, and we all got along well. We spent time at his mom's place and my house. As much as we enjoyed each other, along with the sex, I was beginning to think that Marvin was a user because he was not working and that began to wear on me. We fought through it for several months, and I could no longer deal with it. We went our separate ways, and I allowed no time for myself to heal. Of course, I had no idea what that meant at that time.

As our relationship came to a halt, my friend Terri introduced me to Lloyd in December 1995. She was dating his brother-in-law Arnold, who was incarcerated. He wasn't a looker, but when you don't know who you are and how special you are, you don't care who you are with. The first night we met, I wore my purple sweatsuit because that was his favorite color.

I always catered to what they wanted so that they would want me. I'm sure we had sex, and I stayed the night at his house. This became a regular thing, and before you know it, I pretty much lived there. There is nothing to explain about the relationship as we did nothing but watch movies and have sex, as I was just a convenient hole for him to dump into.

We never went out, and we never did things together or for each other. It bothered me, but I never made a fuss about it because he came back to the house every night. We would talk, but like I said, it wasn't my desire but a touch of attention, so I stayed. I remember one day we were having sex and his mother walked in on us. She came up the stairs and said, "I should pull the covers off of her." He claims that he gave her a key for emergencies only, but she used it when she chose to. I met a few members of his family, but we were hardly around them. It was fast food, or I was eating at my mom's house. There was never food in the house for me to cook. I liked to cook, but there was nothing there.

He claimed that he was always working, but I later found out that he was seeing Carol, to whom he is now married. At this time, I was working for Vasi International and getting calls from Marvin and messages from Marvin. Marvin was in love and wanted us to get back together.

I would get calls from him, his sister and messages with songs on them. I ignored them because I was with Lloyd. We were having sex so often, and me not wanting to get pregnant, I went to the clinic to get on birth control. I made the appointment and arrived at my appointed time. I entered the office, which was located in Edmondson Village. I was not ready for the news I received.

I checked in and waited to be seen. I completed the necessary documentation and answered the general questions that were asked. I turned in the papers, and they requested a urine sample and blood to be tested before they placed me on birth control. I sat in the room patiently waiting for the nurse to return.

When she finally returned to the room, she informed me that they could not provide me with birth control. I looked at her crazy and asked, "Why?" She said, "Ms. Timmons, you are pregnant." I looked at her in disbelief and said that is not possible. She said, "Well, whoever told you that was incorrect." "You are six weeks pregnant, congratulations!" I began to cry. I don't know if I was excited or scared. My mother was no longer here, the person I was pregnant by, I had not known for long, nor was I in love with him, but I knew that abortion was not an option. It had only been a month since my mother had passed away and now I am pregnant. I was provided with a prescription for vitamins and Iron pills. I called Terri first to let her know.

She was excited and told me to call her after talking to Lloyd. I called Lloyd and told him that we needed to talk. He asked about what and I told him we would talk when I saw him. I think I called a few more people before I arrived at Lloyd's place. When I arrived, he was sitting on the steps, and I sat next to him. I looked at him, and I shared the news that I was pregnant. Lloyd was in shock.

He did not look happy at all. I proceeded to tell him how things went. He did not want any more kids, which he clearly did not show by having unprotected sex. When I was done, he asked what I was going to do, and I informed him that I was not sure, but I knew. He got up, got on his bike and left. He went to tell Carol what he was just informed of. Upon his return, he gave me the option to either have an abortion or work on our relationship. Of course, my choice was to have the baby.

I was living in sin and clinically depressed, but I knew that God did not make mistakes. We argued for quite some time, and a few days later, I packed my things and went to stay with my dad, as my uncle was living in my townhome. Lloyd and I had not spoken to one another until after Ceané was born. The only reason it happened then is because we ran into each other a few times at the DMV and he asked about Ceané. We had minimal conversation. The next time he asked about pictures and if he could have them and I allowed him to keep them. We saw each other a few more times, but Ceané did not meet him until she was nine years old.

In the meantime, Marvin and I got back together, and he was quite happy. I was afraid to tell him that I was pregnant, but he said he figured that is what had taken place. I shared everything with him, and he said that he would take the responsibility of being Ceané's father. We attended one of his nephew's birthday parties at Chuck E. Cheese, and that is when we broke the news. Everyone was very excited and could not wait for her to arrive.

My pregnancy was not the greatest as there was too much morning sickness and daddy felt sorry for me, but he helped as much as he could. My daily dinner consisted of Imperial Crab, mixed vegetables, a baked potato, Mrs. Smith Dutch Apple Pie and a gallon of Ruby Red Tangerine drink and anything else I could get my hands on. I worked the night shift, and Marvin worked during the day for UPS. During the pregnancy, I gained thirty-four to thirty-six pounds. I was mostly belly. I did not even have to purchase maternity clothes. I continued to work until I was placed on bedrest.

I attended every prenatal appointment. Ceané's due date was December 31, 1996/1997 and I was excited about possibly having the first baby of the new year. The scariest appointment I faced was when they informed me that Ceané was at high risk of being born with Down Syndrome and they needed to complete amniocentesis. That is when they stick this thin, long needle in your stomach to get a sample of fluid.

Marvin did not attend this appointment with me, but he did go to some appointments with me.

I was scared, and it did not help to see that long needle. I am terrified of needles and get very squeamish. It was a very uncomfortable feeling, and I could not move. They had to be very careful that the needle was placed in the correct spot and not do harm to the baby. They completed the Amnio, and I was told they did not find anything at the next appointment and she should be fine.

I think they complete those tests to see who they can get away with doing it on. I continued to make my appointments to ensure that Ceané was okay, and so was I. Sometime in October, I was placed on bedrest because Ceané was at risk. I was so depressed, and even the beauty that pregnancy signifies could not make me happy. I wanted my mother back, and there was nothing I could do. That was one of the most beautiful and painful times of my life.

I arrived at work one night, not thinking anything of it, only to find that Terri had planned a baby shower for me. I am one of the biggest crybabies, so of course, I cried. Everything was so nice, and that was the only baby shower that I had. Yoshi made her famous mini quiche, and there was a beautiful, delicious cake along with some other goodies. I received gifts from the staff and some of which I still have today. Eventually, I plan to have them framed for Ceané to hang in her home. They made me the cutest little paper plate bonnet from the ribbon taken off the gifts, and we all had a great time. It brought me great joy to know that people cared about me.

I enjoyed the later months of pregnancy, as Ceané grew and my body turned into a beautiful sight. My birthday was coming up, and Marvin made it very special. He told me to pack an overnight bag, which I did. When I arrived at his house, and we were about to leave, he blindfolded me. I tried to get out of it, but that did not work. He drove, and it felt like we drove for miles. We finally arrived at the destination after riding around for almost three hours. We pulled up, and the valet took the car. He grabbed my hand and led me into a building. All I could hear was a piano playing and lots of people. I thought it was a restaurant, but it was not. He put me in place and told me to stay there.

I could hear people saying, "Awe," all around me. He finally came back and took my hand. He told me where to step and what to do. Upon arriving to the room, he told me to stand still, or I would take a long fall. He returned after a few minutes, opened the door and removed the blindfold. I was in awe. There was a path made of candles and rose petals that led to the bedroom, the bathroom, and the living room. It was so beautiful! He had a bottle of sparkling cider chilling and some fruit. He ran a bath for us, and we sipped on the cider during our bath. We talked and just enjoyed each other that evening.

We got out, watched a little TV and began kissing passionately. Of course, kissing turned into intimacy, and it was great even while being pregnant. We fell asleep in each other's arms, and it was a beautiful evening. We returned home the next day and continued to prepare for the baby. It was work as usual and handling the pregnancy. I would wobble all over the place, but I still was missing my mother, and Ceané was not due until December, so we thought.

In the months to come, we would enjoy watching her move from one side to the other. We loved seeing her feet pressed against my stomach or her head moving from side to side in my belly. She would kick and move and loved to eat. I would read to her and place headphones on my tummy so she could listen to music. Yes, I was one of those mothers. She came into the world loving music, which I continued to play for her as well as sing.

On October 27, 1996, around one something in the morning, I started cramping. I had no idea that I was going into labor. I got up and went to the bathroom, and after urinating, I noticed this pink thing (Mucus plug) in the toilet. I was clueless, so I called the hospital, and they informed me that I needed to get there. I woke my dad up, he got dressed, and I called Marvin and told him. He got to my house around two something in the morning. We were on our way to the hospital.

My dad was behind Marvin, who was driving like speed racer. We hit Cooks Lane, and sirens went off. Marvin never stopped, and my dad said the cop gave up because Marvin kept going. We arrived at the emergency room. Marvin jumped out of the car and said loudly, "We got a live one here!" They brought out a wheelchair and rolled me in. They took me to a room to get my vitals and check my cervix. I had already begun to dilate, but they provided me with Magnesium to try and stop the birth.

They placed me in a delivery room in hopes that Ceané would change her mind. I was tired and dozed in and out of sleep. I felt wet at one time but did not pay any attention to it. A little later, I began to toss and turn because I could not sleep, although Marvin was sleeping quite well. I woke him up because the contractions returned and I told Marvin that it felt as if I had to poop. He called a nurse, they came in, checked me and asked if I knew that my water broke and I told them no. The nurse checked my cervix and told me that I was about to give birth.

The mirror was adjusted, the bed broke down, and the doctor called in the room. At 10:41 AM, October 1996, Ceané was born at GBMC. She was born eight weeks early at two pounds and ten ounces. I did not get to engage in the same experience as other mothers in being able to hold their bundle of joy. She was taken immediately, and I heard a physician say, "What's that?" And another one responded, "Herpes." I never thought about it or what that meant, as nothing was said about it. My focus was on the pain and if Ceané was okay. Weeks went by without us being able to hold her. We did not know if she was going to make it. She was hooked up to various machines, her eyes covered and she was extremely small. She was so small that I could cradle her with one hand. I was not allowed to hold her because of her weight and some complications.

When I was finally able to see her, she had tubes coming out of her nose and mouth. She had to remain in the NICU unit until they thought she was well enough to leave if it came to that. She later contracted jaundice, and it was still hard for her to breathe on her own. If I recall correctly, it was a week or two before I could even hold her.

We could touch her hand through the portal holes in the incubator. She had a stream of visitors and some that could not stand to see her being so small with all the tubes she was connected to. My dad and grandmother were two of the many that could not stand seeing her like that. Ceané had an angel for a nurse, and her name was Kim. When Kim was on-site, no one else was allowed to care for her. She treated Ceané as if she was her own. I remember getting a call from Kim one day in a rage. Kim did not work that day, but when she returned, she found that in others trying to find a vein, they shaved off one side of Ceané's hair, which was unnecessary.

I arrived at the hospital already aware, and I was still upset because they had placed the tube in her leg. I fussed a bit, but that would not bring Ceané's hair back any quicker. We prayed and read the Holy Bible to her, and when I left, I turned her tape recorder on where classical and gospel music played. Kim continued to take care of Ceané, and the hospital even treated us to a steak dinner one night as Marvin and I had the evening to ourselves. GBMC is the greatest hospital to give birth at. We enjoyed the night. Our time with her varied, but I was there every moment I could be there. During the day and a few nights, but mostly during the day, as there was nowhere to sleep.

Sometimes I would take Marvin to work and sometimes, he would leave me at the hospital and come back after work. Nurse Kim taught Marvin and me how to care for Ceané. She showed us how to feed, bathe and change her. It was wonderful to see Marvin bathing her, although he was scared. She was picking up weight, and Ceané was released a week before Christmas, and it was the best. I took her home alone as Marvin had to work. This, I can say, was one of the hardest times in my life, as my mother was not there, I was clueless about being a mother, and I was still in a state of depression.

We arrived home, and daddy held her. Marvin would come over after work, or we would go to his house. No one, other than my father, had seen Ceané until Christmas. Christmas eve, we stayed the night at Kishya's house. We milled around as Noel opened his gifts and just had a great morning. Marvin had placed Ceané in a toy car and was pushing her around. That evening we headed to Marvin's auntie's house, where the family was celebrating.

I could hear the excitement through the door. I could hear someone yelling, "The baby is here, the baby is here!" Marvin's sister, Shana, opened the door and reached for Ceané. I told her that she needs to wash her hands first. A lot of people were not happy with me, but I did not care as she was a preemie and could become ill quickly. They all went to wash their hands and came back for the baby. They were all overjoyed, and Ceané was passed around like a baton at a track meet.

She laughed and played, and everyone smiled as they held the little miracle bundle. We ate and enjoyed family until it was time to leave. It was getting late, and I did not want to have her out late. We took her home, and Marvin returned to his house. I was off for another month due to her arriving early. I returned to work, missing her tremendously.

Marvin would come to the house, and we would watch TV and play with her. My father would accuse Marvin and me of having sex when we were just watching TV or trying to get her to sleep. Upon her falling asleep, he would leave. We would go to his mom's house sometime as he would keep Ceané or we would have sex there. Our relationship began to fall apart eventually. I fell into post-partum depression heavily. I began not to trust Marvin and felt bad about myself all the time.

I took care of Ceané the best I could in my mental state, but it was not enough. After a few months, Marvin and I split up, and he told me we needed to talk. He said that he met someone in New York and they were going to have a baby, so he needed to tell his family that Ceané was not his. The end of this conversation led us both to tears. We cried in the back of my car for quite some time before we departed from one another. We did not talk anymore after that. His family was hurt, but his father told me that I could not change her name and that she will always be a Batten as long as she lives.

Mr. B. and his fiancé continued to love on Ceané just like he said he would. They would purchase a new dress for her almost every holiday, along with toys and an Easter basket.

She would spend weekends with them, and they would have lots of fun. Mr. B. would also discipline Ceané, which contributed to her being a standup human being. I made sure I informed him of everything that took place in her life, good and bad. Again, lust and perversion are spirits that you are opened up to when molested.

One of the most challenging relationships to sever was with another female. She was a great friend who turned into someone I became sexually involved with.

Dealing with rejection was already hard. However, dealing with betrayal, lust, and lack of trust in relationships left me lonely. Erica was one of the top designers in Maryland. She created beautiful couture fashion designs. I met her after one of her shows because I wanted to purchase a few of her garments and speak with her about possibly showcasing her designs in my show. We came to be friends after I auditioned to become one of her models. I then matriculated to becoming her model trainer as well. When you saw her, you saw me and then we became family. I participated in the shows and we hung out together. For the most part, it was a great relationship. When she created a new line, she would invite me over to help myself to the previous line. We spent a lot of time together and so much so that we did things for one another and our families. There was a time she needed to get away, so I supplied the resources so she could do so. I never asked for anything. However, that was just me. I love making people happy. So much so, I also purchased a cell phone for her. She had a business, along with kids and I thought it was necessary.

The betrayal and hurt came in when Erica told someone that I was not diagnosed with cancer but HIV. She spread that rumor, and I was truly hurt. I found out through someone who received a phone call from a mutual friend. I was there for her not just financially but also as a sounding board. Being that sounding board led to deeper things. When I say deeper things, I'm speaking of another side of our relationship, lust. What began as a mutual sister-friend relationship, turned into lust. I will save you the details but know that I enjoyed her and wanted more. Wanting more turned into another experience and the betrayal and lust was already embedded. I wasn't emotionally and spiritually aware enough to know what was taking place.

This relationship caused a deeper issue of pain, hurt, despair and loneliness. It also made me stop helping and wanting to help people. It took a long time for me to heal from this relationship.

Never let your past be so heavy that you stop trying to find yourself, loving yourself, and knowing the truth about how the enemy works. He will send it 90% the way that you like it.

Please know that counseling can be the best thing you could ever do for yourself. Give yourself time to heal, time to breathe, time to get to know yourself all over again. When we get into relationships, we tend to lose ourselves because we want to keep our mate happy. So we do everything in our power to make sure that they get everything they want and need.

As humans, we get involved in relationships that are no good for us. We want to be loved and cared for. Can you think of a relationship where you asked yourself, "Who is this person I am in relationship with and why do I need to get out of it?

Questions

What relationship made you say, "That is the final straw! I need to get my life together. I know my worth!"

_____

_____

_____

_____

How were you manipulated to remain in a relationship that you knew was harmful to you? Why did you stay?

_____

_____

_____

_____

What relationships do you need to relinquish today to become healthy? (It could be a family member, a love interest, or a childhood friend) What plan do you have in place to leave?

_____

_____

_____

_____

How does the abuse you suffered affect your life today?

_____

_____

_____

_____

You Got This!

A boxer is paid millions of dollars to get punched on. You are not a sparring partner, a sex slave or a trash can for people to dump into. You are valuable; you are loved, and you are an amazing human being who has so much to offer the world. Hey, do you know that others are watching you? Do you know that others are waiting for you to walk away from your past so you can help them step into their future? They are waiting for you to walk away from the pain and past. The moment you walk away, they will begin thinking about how they can walk away from everything so the healing process can begin. They want the same peace, joy, and happiness that you now have. Be the beacon of light you were born to be. Break the abuse off your life. Be the hero for others that you needed. Heaven has your back and guess what? So do

Chapter 4

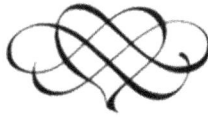

Unfit to be anyone's Mother or Wife– The Unclean Truth

I remember dancing at two parties which allowed me to live the somewhat dream of being a "Luke" dancer. The Two Live Crew was a rap group who had sexy music videos with girls that had very curvaceous bodies and vulgar lyrics. I wanted the attention. I was provided that opportunity when I began stripping for private parties.

The first party I remember dancing at was for someone named Bryan. This party was brought to my attention by my friend Jackie. Jackie was a hustler at a young age and dealt more with males than females. She was like security for me. When we hung out, and I did not want to dance with someone, Jackie made sure he understood that I said no and meant it. I don't remember how much money I made that night, but I was told that I was the best dancer there even without all the tricks that the other dancers performed. I was the first girl to perform, and I was quite nervous.

I had a drink before I went out to calm my nerves, as I had never danced like this before. I danced on and around him, and he seemed to be pleased, but who would not when you have a half- naked girl dancing on your lap? I danced for about fifteen minutes before heading back to the room, where I got dressed and sat on the bed. I felt dirty and ashamed. But why? This was something new to me. Honestly, I did not need the money, but it was easily earned. Bryan had several other dancers perform for him before he came back to the room where we engaged in sex. The message was relayed to me that even with all the other tricks that the girls performed, he enjoyed my routine the best. I guess it was the best because he received extra attention from me. I was so easily influenced and naïve about life.

After that night, I was offered more opportunities to dance, but I declined. I was introduced to a lot of guys through Jackie. Maurice was another person I met through her and began prostituting myself to. We would meet up every Saturday, he would pay me, and I would do anything he wanted me to. We would have sex for hours. Maurice was a client for quite a while.

There were many others, but the relationships were different. We did not exchange money for sex. Sometimes we would exchange goods. Whether it was handbags, jewelry, shoes, or electronics, it was still prostitution, with a different type of exchange.

Don't allow yourself to be fooled. Reflect on some of the relationships you were in. What did you exchange sex for; Louboutin, Chanel, Michael Kors, Fendi, Gucci, tickets to a concert, or maybe dinner?

I remember one large party I did for this guy Mike in a hall. I didn't make much money because there were so many other girls there. I remember going back to his house and having sex with him. He was older, and I allowed it to happen. We went inside of his home, and he began touching me. If I only knew the power of the word "no" and stop in those days, there is no telling where I would be.

It was one of the most disgusting times of my life. I could not wait for it to be over so I could go home. I remember going to my house and being in the shower and bath for such a long time, trying to wash the filth off. After that, I disconnected myself from him. I would see him and hold my head down in shame. I subjected myself to much destructive behavior. I often wonder how different my life would be if the dynamics of my family were different. If loved properly and a firm foundation in Jesus was laid, I wonder if my life would have taken a different path.

Rejection was already an issue in my family, although I didn't realize it until later in life. There was and is so much greatness on my family, but because no one ever broke or reversed the generational curses, hurt, disappointment and abuse continued throughout our bloodline. Due to my abuse, I was already living in rejection, but it was stronger over the life of Ceane before she was even born. Upon finding out I was pregnant, Ceane's father had stated he wanted me to abort her, so we could work on our relationship. In my eyes, it was a lack thereof. I was either at work or at his house, alone. It was more a sexual partnership than a relationship. With her father wanting me to have an abortion and then me not giving her 100% of what she needed, it seemed that her life was already set to fail. In learning more about spirits, you discover they enter in various ways. The enemy was out for Ceané before she was even born. She was never supposed to be born or live when she arrived. Through all of this, we both survived.

What I thought should have been one of the happiest times of my life was not. She was beautiful, born as a preemie and, for the most part, always happy, but I wasn't. My mother deceased, my grandmother only interested in benefitting from my mother's death and the family is no longer close. I felt as if I was alone, even with the beautiful gift that God bestowed upon me. Ceané was not given the life she deserved, and I wish I could change it.

Post-partum depression is no joke, and it does not help that my mother committed suicide the month before I found out I was pregnant. Ceané arrived, and I was so happy, so I thought. After informing 'her donor,' as I so fondly called him, we ended up moving in with my dad. I moved out of the donor's house, as my Uncle Jamie was living in my townhome, which I lost, shortly after that because he could not afford it and left me with a $3,000 BG&E bill. He also took all my belongings and moved them without telling me. Every time I would ask him to take me there, he always made an excuse.

Okay, enough about him. Ceané and I moved in with my dad and Marvin, who I became reacquainted with, due to his persistence, opted to take on the role of Ceané's father. After she was born and released from the hospital, he would come over and spend time with us, and we would go to his mom's house and spend time there. We were becoming quite the little family, but I was suffering from post-partum depression and deemed clinically depressed. Ceané brought joy to everyone, but I was not happy, as well as empty. I was taking meds for depression but had to stop due to breastfeeding. Those pills had me walking around like a zombie.

I was trying my best to be a good mother and still failed. I asked my aunt to keep Ceané for a little while due to recording some music, but I was not fit to raise her and could not handle taking care of her. I can't even recall who I was seeing at the time, which meant I was probably jumping from man to man.

I provided all that Ceané needed and visited her on the weekends, and she was gone for about a month or so. I missed her so much, but she deserved better than what I could offer her at that time. My auntie and cousin helped me tremendously until Kim came into the picture. Ceané was a toddler, and that helped me a lot. Kim kept her clean, completed her homework with her, took her to school and made sure she was fed. I loved her the best I knew how, but even that wasn't good enough.

She wanted for nothing but love. The love I could provide was limited because I didn't love myself. I remember me picking her up from Philadelphia, and all I kept seeing was me driving into a wall with her and killing us both. Just imagine if that would have happened, this book would not have been written and she would not be flourishing into a scientist. In the years to come, as Ceané was growing up, we moved to multiple places. We went from a three-bedroom apartment into a one-bedroom apartment, which became roach-infested and dirty. I would not clean up, and there were days when Ceané would come home talking about how the kids were speaking of the roach crawling around the classroom. She had an idea it was from her backpack. She had no right growing up in that environment, but I was dirty, lazy and pitiful.

I remember she would ask me to play with her, and I would always say, "Not right now" or "later," and those times would never come. I said the same things when she was hungry. All I wanted to do was sleep. Looking back, I wish I would have been in better health so that I could play house and dolls with her and teach her how to cook meals and hang out and do things. She deserved so much better and getting through depression helped me to do better. It was I who taught Ceané how to be unclean. It was I who taught her how to be lazy.

I wanted so much for her, but I had no idea of how to give it or teach it to her. I was made to do so many grown-up things at an early age that I did not want to do them when I became an adult. The only thing it seemed that I liked doing was receiving attention, and most of that came along with having sex. I taught her how to clean, but it was not enforced. I never wanted to be on her bad side, which meant I felt more like a friend than her parent.

I know that I also performed some parental duties, because it seemed that she was more upset with me, instead of trying to build a better relationship. Honestly, her younger days were the best. We would get dressed up to take our almost weekly photo shoot, she was in Ballet, and I introduced her to so many things. Her granddad and his girlfriend did the same.

He would pick Ceané up almost every weekend and please don't let it be a holiday. Ceané always spoke of how much fun she had with granddad and Zia. She raved about the Cinnamon/sugar toast Zia would make and them baking cookies. I was happy that she was being exposed to various things that made her happy and kept her looking beautiful.

Her granddad was always on her about the boys, and that granddad was her only boyfriend. The older she became, the more serious he was and the funnier it became to her. I appreciated the relationship they had. Even when his son told him that Ceané was not his, he said, "I do not care. She will always be a Batten." To this day, they still have a very beautiful relationship.

Another reason I felt that I was unfit was that I would leave my precious baby home alone to go lay up with someone I did not even want to be with. I was damaged, broken, and a great big ole mess. I was looking for love, affection, and attention in all the wrong places. I met someone on my job, whom I should have never been with. He was smooth with his approach, and I fell for it. I later found out he was married. He dated the director who ran our floor, and I was told they were trying to rekindle their relationship, but I thought nothing of it.

I was in a desperate place, and I wanted someone. I was not even attracted to him, but he dressed nice and smelled good, along with being a habitual liar. I believe he was in the separation stage of getting a divorce. I would pick Ceané up from school or daycare, feed her, bathe her and wait for her to fall asleep before I went to be with him. Anything could have happened to her, and it would have been all my fault.

I stayed the night with him almost every night. He cooked, and we would watch tv or talk. We never went out together except for when we first met. I met one of his friends, but we will talk about that later. We slept on an air mattress for quite some time. It continued to puzzle me why he wanted us to get a place together when he claimed that he owned a home. The home that he spoke of was posted in his cube. It was a printout and not an actual picture. I did find out from someone that knew him quite well; he never owned the house. He liked it a lot.

There is nothing wrong with dreaming, but when you try to be something that you are not, it all comes to light. It did dawn on me later that no one in their right mind that owned a home would pay rent for an apartment unless they had something to hide or it was easier to get another place that was closer to work for them instead of commuting. Speaking of right mind, I was not in mine. Trolloping behind him, because my gut told me he was no good, I was out of it. He would lie about having to go to DC to visit another co-worker, only to find out that was his way of getting rid of me so he could have other women or his friends come over to the apartment.

The apartment was in a nice high-rise building overlooking the city, but unfurnished. In my time with him, several eviction notices were left on the door, which he thought I never saw. I had a key in the beginning, but I guess because I would not sign the lease, I was no longer privileged to do so. We had some fun times, but also some not so fun times. The one night that changed everything was one of the nights he lied about having to go out of town, only for me to go to the apartment and overhear him talking to the director.

Yes, I did not trust him, but because of my mental and emotional state, I would not leave either. They were laughing and giggling about how something at work was not a rule, but she, along with my boss at the time, was trying to get rid of me. I knocked on the door, and it got quiet. It took several minutes for him to answer and he slid out so I would not see her. We talked, and he told me that he was trying to find out for me, why they were trying to get rid of me. I was so hurt, but I continued to listen to the lie.

We went into a stairwell, as I began to get upset. Our voices grew louder, and I started to hit him in the face and head with my keys. I drew blood. I left the area but waited for her to leave, which was hours later. He called me, and of course, I went upstairs, and we made up. I returned to work, telling those that I talked to what happened. Of course, it spread through the building like wildfire. I did not care.

I was a woman scorned and on the verge of mentally losing it. We remained together for a while longer until it just did not make sense anymore.

Although in a broken state, I knew I deserved better. There was more to this story, as one day on the elevator at work, an administrator said, "I told her to stop sleeping with her staff." I looked and said, wow.

I had no clue that I had a nervous breakdown until I went to see my physician. I was placed on medication and could not return to work. I was now in therapy trying to heal, but I knew that would not last forever. I did my best to make sure that Ceané was straight with school and I was there for her as much as I could be. I wish I could do it all over again and be the mother she needed and deserved me to be. There is a saying, "When you know better, you do better." When you don't know how abuse affects your life, there is no telling where it will take you. Needless to say, our relationship ended, and I was on my way to being healed.

With her last year in middle school, where she consistently made the honor roll and was inducted into the 'Honor Society,' I was looking to move to Howard County, as they are one of the wealthiest counties in Maryland. The education system is always at the top of the country, not just the state, but the country. An application was already placed with the housing department, but a new apartment complex was built in the county and needless to say, I was approved for one of them.

With everything going on at my job, I was also trying to find employment in Howard County, which would help so much with everything else. This place was much cleaner, larger and comfortable. Ceané had her own room and bathroom. We were on opposite sides of the house.

Moving was tough for Ceané because the city was all she knew. That is where her friends were and what she connected to the most. I was so hard on Ceané, only because I wanted so much more for her than my parents gave me. I allowed my mom not being here, become a horrible excuse as to why I did not raise Ceané properly. I let my lack of self-love stop me from doing things that I wanted to share with her and teach her.

It became evident that over time, she was a very strong-willed person. I would try to tell her things, but it was always, "I know." Then as soon as the outcome was different or she needed help which she readily denied, she came back to me for the answer. God would always set it up, but she failed to see it. I would try to impart to her, but she rejected my advice and would do it her way. It would not even take a full hour before I was receiving a phone call or text.

The conversation would always deal with what I was trying to share with her from the very beginning. God would send her back, maybe as a way of humiliation or getting her to see that I did know what I was talking about or perhaps even to trust me. There was so much damage done to her, not just by her father, but by me as well. Sometimes scared to impart or make suggestions, I would remain silent. It became so frequent that I just stopped.

I figured she knew everything, so I stop offering. It was funny how God turned it around. It later came to the point where she would give her usual response, and it would backfire in her face, and guess who she came to, to bail her out, moi. It became such a thing, I stopped allowing it to bother me and would say, "Okay, God has a funny sense of humor. Let's see how this will play out.

There were times, I did not want to deal, but I refused to allow her to be disrespectful. One confrontation I remember us having led to me believing that she ran away. I searched everywhere, called her friend's home, but nothing. After several hours, I called the police, only to find her laying in her room, almost under her bed, with the largest kitchen knife next to her. I can't recall if she was considering killing herself or trying to kill me if I came near her.

She stayed punished, and as I look back, it was mostly because she was rebelling. I also did not find out until she went to college that she had been molested by a friend of the family's brother, a designer that I had worked with son and by the daycare provider, Ms. Sappington's son, whom she sold candy for and was with quite frequently.

As time progressed, things between her and I became better. Ceané even thanked me later for moving to Columbia so that she could receive a better education. She also said she wished we would have moved sooner. Ceané completed high school and graduated. Things shifted between us as we began to communicate more and spent more time together. I learned so much during this time, and it helped me to become a better person.

A compliment was always given as to how well-mannered and beautiful she was. She was trying to figure out where that was taking place because she mumbled under her breath and talked back to me. I remember on several occasions giving her the backhand that my mother gave me. I did not hit her as hard though.

The difficulty of our relationship continued to diminish as she was preparing to leave for college. I was so proud of her. I did not provide Ceané with the encouragement and the validation that she needed because I did not know how to provide it and that it was something I was supposed to do. I offered as much support as I knew how to. I gave parties to show how proud of her and how much I did appreciate her.

She had a party for almost every birthday, her graduation, as well as heading off to college. The older she became, the better we became with each other. Our relationship dynamics have changed for the better. Our communication has shifted, although we still have a lot of work to do. We share more and occasionally have date nights. To this day, we continue to work towards a better relationship and building a mother-daughter relationship that is conducive to what God called it to be.

Questions

Was there anyone or anything that ever made you feel unfit? Answer the questions below to help you have a clearer picture of who and what you need to sever from your life.

Who or what made you feel that you were unfit?

_____

_____

_____

_____

What baggage are you carrying around that is keeping you in bondage?

_____

_____

_____

_____

What communication skills do you need to sharpen so that what you say is clear?

_____

_____

_____

_____

What are some of the repeating patterns you see in your relationships?

_____

_____

_____

_____

What characteristics would you like your ideal relationships to have?

_____

_____

_____

_____

You Got This!

The power of a woman can't be defined in words, the power unbelievable, the character speaks in volumes, and the mass of strength is formed from the name woman.

Chapter 5

Empty, Broken and Gifted

Say it with me, "I have purpose!" Now, repeat it until you believe it. We were all blessed with gifts from God. It may be one or many. In a previous chapter, I talked about how being abused skews your perception of everything. Sexual abuse steals portions of your soul and your creative flow. You believe you are worthless and you have no purpose. There were promises God made to you, but you don't see any sign of light or manifestation anywhere. There seems to be a dark cloud hovering over you no matter where you go or what you do. Naturally, there are things you are phenomenal at doing, but the glimmer of hope doesn't allow you to be creative. I did not realize all the blessings and value of my life until I began to heal. I reflected on my life to see how blessed I was with many gifts and talents, and so are you. I want to help you understand how everything you need is in you and that when you have been violated and word curses have been spoken over you, you do not think much of yourself at all. You think of yourself as below average. And those gifts may go to waste because you don't believe that you can accomplish anything. How many times as a child were you asked, "What do you want to be when you grow up?" My answer was always, "A stuntwoman, an opera singer, a model, and an actress." Did I become any of them, not the way I intended. But I dabbled in some of them. I am now aware of what I am capable of and plan to use every gift and talent.

I could sing, dance, model, a naturally fast runner, played instruments, produced fashion shows, was a natural encourager; I could act and do this very thing which you're holding in your hand, write. I left so many things on the table due to the lack of confidence and love for myself. If I was focused on my healing instead of who I could keep between my legs, there is no telling where I would be now. Abuse affects every area of your life. Once you realize it, you must be willing to work hard and fight for your life. Yes, I said fight. You may not have to fight physically anymore, but the necessity to fight verbally is a necessity to overcome the darkness and walk through healing. You need clarity in order to take an inventory of what you're capable of and how capable you are of doing it.

My first love was for the fashion industry. I have played many roles in the local fashion industry as well as professionally. I began modeling and competing in pageants around the age of 4, maybe 5. Winning pageants lead to wearing pretty gowns and riding in parades through

Manning, South Carolina. I loved smiling and waving at all the people. Due to returning to Baltimore, I was removed from that environment.

I was reintroduced to modeling in my teenage years but on a larger scale. In my senior year, one of my instructors and I co-created a charm club. It was created to assist in building self-esteem and learning proper etiquette. It made me feel great because I was not accepted overall in school. Even today, there are still classmates that do not interact with me. I was the captain of the Pom-Pom squad, a choir member and ran track and field. But I was not liked much by my team members. On the outside, people believed I had high self-esteem, and some thought I was arrogant. If they only knew the trauma that I was living through.

In my dress and my actions, I was crying out for attention. All we ever want is to be loved and accepted by people. My schoolmates had no idea of the 'other life' I was living. I had been molested and was trying to figure out who I was and where I fit in. Not knowing where, I just flowed with everything and never questioned it. In that hurtful place of unacceptance, I learned of another gift, singing.

I sang with my aunt for fun, but I was ignorant of the true gift that God gave me. The gift of singing was nurtured at Edmondson-Westside High School through Ms. Gardner, our music teacher. She saw something in me and prompted me to perform one year in the school's talent show. I performed my first solo singing a part of 'My Country Tis of Thee,' as well as performing a comedic rendition of Little Richard, from the

1988 Grammy Awards. Afterward, many students provided accolades because that was the first time they ever heard or saw me perform. I was terrified, but I loved being on stage.

The following year, I graduated from high school and returned to modeling. It started with attending Nhoj Cassir's School of Modeling. It was fun but costly. What I did gain from them was the pleasure of meeting Robert Mercer, a modeling instructor, with whom I'm still friends. Getting to know Robert was great. However, it was time to take my talent elsewhere, due to the lack of opportunity with Nhoj Cassir's school. Unlike Cassir's school, Odyssey Modeling School provided a wide array of opportunities. I learned a lot, met a broad span of people, and traveled to other states to perform.

Under the instruction of Bentley Wallace, Wesley Alton, Romero Johns, Joseph Pugh and Ms. George, we learned how to apply make-up, walk the catwalk, proper etiquette tips and acting. Romero took me under his wings and taught me more than I could ever imagine. He also made me a part of his family, and they loved me, especially his mother, Noni. I spent a lot of time with Romero and his family.

I started picking up more shows and photoshoots. I begin creating online portfolios to gain more exposure. I met photographers and learned what I could, but it started going in a different direction. I met a photographer by the name of Eric, who I would shoot with often. I was still young and very naïve. I was very trusting of any and everyone.

Needless to say, one day, I found myself shooting nudes with Eric. It was something he suggested, and I thought it would be okay but don't ask me why. I know rejection played a part. I wanted to be liked and accepted so I would continue to receive free photographs. I don't recall ever saying no to anyone because I wanted them to continue to like me. Eric and I continued to shoot together, until one day, I decided against it. I never heard from Eric again, and I was okay with that.

What happened is that I was beginning to feel better about myself. Perhaps my conscience was getting the best of me. I never allowed anyone to photograph me in the nude again after that. Something inside of me was changing, though it was still a struggle. I wanted to be liked and loved, but not in that manner. I found myself turning down offers for shows and photo sessions. I still loved what I was doing but looking at it from a different perspective.

Not only was I still modeling, but dancing for 'Miss Tony.' I was always scandalous in dress to get attention. I began to spend a lot of time with Romero and Anthony. My first performance was at 'Hammerjacks,' which was a local club. It was fun, as we also performed at 'Fantasies,' but the real performance was the night we traveled to 'Tracks' in DC to perform after the 'LGBT March on Washington.' The club was packed, and the music was booming. I had on a two-piece crochet outfit which was similar to a bikini and some boots. Pumpin Paul and another dancer, along with myself, performed behind Tony. That night Rupurt was hosting the event, but not in drag. I met a lot of people that night and had a blast. Dancing provided this electric feeling that I never wanted to leave. I was heavy on the LGBT scene because I was still lost and that is where I was being embraced for being the best me that I knew how to be. I was happy in that arena due to being embraced, loved on and supported in such an epic manner.

A few more shows and I was no longer dancing with Tony. Nothing was wrong. He just decided to go with all-male dancers. We remained friends and Paul, and I spoke quite often. Can we just say it was God! Due to my attention deficit, it was time to move on. God was trying to reel me in closer to him, but I kept doing me. The attention I was receiving felt so good because it wasn't putting me in danger. Just understand that low self-esteem kept me seeking attention, whether it was good or bad. I never stopped modeling though. I did it for many others. If I ever began a project and things did not work out, I always returned heavily to modeling.

My gifts and talents allowed me once again to meet some amazing people. One of those people was Marquis. We met at a model call for a hair show. Marquis and I began hanging out and later, he became my hairstylist and makeup artist. Marquis was very creative and fun. We participated in fashion shows together. We went to amusement parks and clubs to dance and walk the night away. I would often tag along with Marquis when he performed as a female impersonator.

He was absolutely the best at everything he did. Marquis and I were so close that Ceané and I were invited to his family's home for Thanksgiving, but we never went. I was suffering from the abuse in such a way that I did not like getting close to families due to thinking I would be hurt again. When you get accustomed to people walking out of your life on a regular basis, it becomes a scary situation and you self-sabotage. Marquis was the reason for my being published in hair magazines, although they were not my first. Marquis really helped me to become a better person because he was always so encouraging.

Fashion allowed me to take on roles other than modeling. I was great at it, which allowed me to train models for designers. I was honored to be able to impart what I had learned over the years. I hated rehearsals. If you truly call yourself a model, you should not have to rehearse, but have a run-through on the day of the show. Felicia Dietrich and Erica Sams were the first designers to grant me the privilege of training models. I will forever be grateful to them both for the opportunity. I later trained models who signed with major modeling agencies.

During my time in school, I was told I should go into journalism, as well as work in the voiceover field. I never took it seriously, but as I write this, I reflect on how my voice has been used. I laid down vocals for many recordings, but they were never used. I worked on solo and group projects. Vocal coaches pushed me and informed me that my range was equivalent to musical greats. The difference is that I did not pursue music like they did.

I met Phil online, and he owned his own studio. We met just to talk to see where we could take this and what we could do with it. We both concluded that this could be something special. I literally went into the recording booth immediately. This was when I began to write my own music. It is amazing that, when you have gone through so much hurt, it is easy to write. Writing lyrics produced a sense of healing for me.

I don't know what it is about putting pen to paper, but it is refreshing and a major release. I completed 3-4 songs, and we recorded them, as well as some others that Phil had. After a while of working solo, I partnered with another vocalist who had a beautiful voice. She wasn't the first nor the last. Although we produced great music together, we parted ways.

As I placed my love for singing on the back burner, I returned to modeling. I began working with the likes of Felicia Dietrich. I came in as a model and soon matriculated to her model trainer, as well as handling other duties, so she could focus on creating beautiful and unique garments. Our relationship transpired from professional to family in a short time frame.

Even in this, God was showing me that he had instilled so much in me. I did not realize at that time I was a teacher.

I always loved encouraging others and pushing them to see how great they are. I never understood why I was so obsessed with things being done the correct way. I loved reading about etiquette and utilizing it. Who would have ever thought this broken little girl would have a great influence on people of all ages.

I met and began to model with Robert in 2004. I was responding to a model call, and I made the cut. From then on, I performed at just about every show he produced. Due to him being so creative, he later matriculated from just producing high-quality fashion shows to opening a school where he taught modeling. A curriculum was created to include modeling, acting, etiquette and a fashion show for the graduating class. I taught a segment of the modeling class, along with the etiquette course. I met many great families and loved working with Robert. The parents were learning along with their children. The school received rave reviews. Robert also was the creative director for 'Ripped Genes, a successful male calendar Robert created. Years later, the female version, 'Ripped Janes, was created, in which I was published two years straight.

Even in modeling, I was hard on myself. That becomes an issue when you deal with so many things. When you are not sure of who you are, how valuable you are and the many gifts, talents and worth you bring to things, you will unnecessarily drive yourself insane.

Some of my family members, such as my great-grandmother, told me once that I was ugly. That stuck with me. She did not realize how it damaged me. I found myself reading more about changing the state of my mind, reading the Bible more so that I could find out who God created me to be. I finally realized that no matter how different we all look, no one is better than the other, but we are all great within ourselves. I had to begin to look at myself the way that God saw me and what He saw was beautiful. In realizing how talented and beautiful I was within myself, the more I began to see it.

I would stand in front of the mirror and say, "Retta Timmons, you sure are beautiful, and don't let anyone ever tell you any different." I began to speak highly of myself but not in conceit. We were all created to be uniquely and distinctly different. I embraced my moles, my shortness, my sexy petite figure, my unique plethora of gifts and decided I was worth it.

In every trial or tribulation you face, never sell yourself short. You have been blessed to touch the lives of many people. Just accept yourself for who you are and embrace everything about yourself. You have been provided with gifts and talents to use as only you know how. Just remember that because other people may have a similar story or the same gifts, no one can do what you do how you do it. It is all unique to who God created you to be.

Now, with all the gifts and talents, I am sure that there is nothing that I can't do. In Philippians 4:13, it says, "I can do all things through Christ which strengthens me." I now know that I can put together events. I can style myself. I can serve others, while they focus on their craft. I've even begun singing again, so we will see where that goes. Right now, it's nothing like singing to God and not focusing on how I sound. Honestly, God loves to hear our voices, so why not use them. I don't know if I will ever do any more acting, but there is definitely more writing in my future. So, let's look at what your gifts and talents are and why aren't you using them?

Questions

Let's complete a quick assessment of gifts and talents. Do you know what yours are? Complete the questions below to see if you know and if you are using them.

What gifts and talents do you have? What are the things you like to do that you would do every day, even if it was for free? What are the unique things that come naturally for you to do?

_____

_____

_____

_____

When was the last time you used them? What business could you build using them?

_____

_____

_____

_____

How can you use them on a daily basis?

_____

_____

_____

_____

You Got This!

There is not one, but multiple things you can do. You have natural gifts and talents that are either hidden, or you are not aware of them yet. That dream that you wanted to achieve since you were a child is still there. You just need boldness, some help, and a plan to make it come true. Don't you dare say you are not capable or you are too old!

There are people in their 90's earning college degrees. So, please don't use that excuse. Go, seek out someone that does it, or jump on the World Wide Web and see how much information you can find on what you love to do. So what ten other people are doing it? They are not you and will not do what you do, how you do it. Don't you dare compare yourself because you are wonderfully, fearfully and uniquely made. NO ONE can do what you do the way you do it. What are you waiting for? Get moving! Destiny is waiting for you.

Chapter 6

Moving Into a Healthy Place- The Emergence of Always Retta

Healing looks different to every individual. Some of us may have a small boo-boo where a band-aid and some Neosporin are all we need. Others need to have surgery to be healed correctly. I needed open heart and spiritual surgery. Like the woman with the issue of blood, we all have something that we have been dealing with and need to find the source of our healing.

Unlike that woman, I had many issues: abandonment, rejection, self-rejection, sexual addiction, attention deficit, word curses, poverty mindset, depression, unforgiveness, hopelessness, lust, perversion, molestation, and oppression. The healing process was lengthy, tiresome and made me wonder what took me so long to begin it. The healing process is healthy, strengthening, and necessary.

You have to be willing and ready to walk into your healing. It takes work and true dedication. The spirit of rejection, abandonment, low self-esteem, attention deficit, Leviathan, and many others, had attached themselves to me. I was a walking bomb waiting to explode due to everything that I had endured in life. Healing was not something that happened overnight for me. It took many years because I had so many spirits dwelling in me. The healing process began at Actout Ministries. It took lots of altar time, many hours of prayer, consecration, and reading. It also took the knowledge of being aware and willing to do what was necessary to get rid of it.

Yes, I was abused sexually, which led to many things. I had been in church all my life. But I was rambunctious and rebellious. I wanted the change but did not want to do the work to get there. I thought that if I just prayed, it would go away. I used God like He was a genie in a bottle. I would even try to bargain with God. "God, if you give me this, I will never do that again."

Some healing came by hearing the word and some came from spending time on the altar so that I could be delivered from some things. The true healing began after I shared my testimony with another church member about being molested. After discussing it the first time, I was able to do so with others. The more I spoke about it, the more guilt, shame, and fear fell off of me. I still cried at times while sharing, but as I gained strength, the tears would stop. In telling my story,

I realized that I was not the only one. Some of the people I confided in became a support system as they were also victims of abuse.

I am unsure of what my purpose was at Actout Ministries, but I knew what it was not. Even in the healing process, I experienced hurt again. Things that I shared with the pastor were talked about from the pulpit. I was told, non-directly, that I could not dance or pray. I was abandoned and unsupported at an event that the ministry asked me to produce. Although the word was helping me to heal, I had to do more. I wanted to know who God was for myself. I would hear things to share with others, but I was scared to say anything and move at the very moment it was heard. I began to sing again, which also brought healing into my life. I was told that I always needed to surround myself with music, and I did.

Due to the damage that was done to me by my pastor, it was time to leave. I needed to deal with and get over my past so that I could move forward. Mother Allen was someone that I met at AM, and she became a big part of my family. She told me about this amazing pastor I should check out. I genuinely believe this was a part of her destiny because after getting me to Destiny Christian Church, she left a few weeks later.

Ceané and I remained at Destiny. I joined the church with tears streaming down my face in two weeks. I will never forget Bishop saying, "That is how I like to see them come." This was new, and DCC was filled with so much love. We were baptized later that day, and it brought such a sense of peace. God was moving, but there was something deep down inside fighting me. The more I attended church, the more I grew. I still had issues which were deep, and that is where I began to learn about demons.

We all have them. They may be generational or just assigned to us. I had both as a result of what I had endured as a child, and I could not let go. I was not holding on purposely, but when you don't know about something, there is no way of fixing it. We are spirit beings wrapped in flesh, so that is what we are up against spirits. I had many of them that were born out of the abuse, some that were spoken over me, and some that had been attached to my family for decades.

What I also learned is that I have so much to say, but the enemy wants to keep my mouth closed, which is why I had such a hard time praying or studying. So, for me, I had to get back to singing. I had to find my *heart song*, if you will. Those songs helped me to increase my faith, praise and worship God and they made me feel better.

In the process of healing, you must be completely honest with yourself. Often, I tried to forget the things I had done because I was ashamed and ridden with guilt. Again, what is written above is just a touch of what I endured. There were many others I laid with. For some of them, I did not even know their last names. But when you lay with someone, your spirits are entangled until you repent and the soul ties are broken.

You have to come face to face with the good, the bad, and the ugly of it all. I cannot tell you the order in which my demons were released because there were so many and some of them are hard to get rid of. Healing was taking place slowly but surely and all the while, I was still living in sin. The lust and perversion spirits were very heavy upon my life. I was still involved with various men, but more focused on being with one at a time. I was focused on the wrong man. I needed to be focused on God.

Building a relationship with God was becoming more important to me, and I needed to find out more about him and what he had for me. I did grow at Actout Ministries, but my growth became pronounced at Destiny Christian Church. DCC was filled with love, hope, and a pastor who cared for his people. As I said earlier, part of my healing came through singing. I joined the praise and worship ministry at DCC, which allowed me to continue to sing praises and worship God from the heart.

Now, I wasn't the greatest singer, but I genuinely sang what I felt and enjoyed doing so. A member pulled me aside one Sunday and told me to never stop singing because I really looked as if I enjoyed it. His words blessed me. I also joined the choir when it was formed. I found myself singing quite a bit. Getting to know God and being obedient was a task for me.

My story had not been shared with a lot of people. This was new territory for me, and I was not sure where this would lead. I attended service faithfully until I began to date a man named Cletus. I remember I was about to leave service one night, when Bishop Nelson said, "Oh, you're putting furniture before God!" I was still putting men before God. Of course, I tried to twist it around, and that was exactly what I was doing. I was still in a broken place, but I was open to chastisement. I think I ended up leaving anyway. If I missed church, I would get an attitude, because that is how much I enjoyed attending. I learned many lessons and did my best to apply them, but something was not clicking for me. No matter how hard I would try to do better, I always reverted to my bad habits.

It is said that it takes thirty days to do something before it becomes a habit, but that did not work for me. I would either quit midway or would complete the thirty days and still return to what I didn't want to be doing. The one great thing is that I was no longer casually sleeping with multiple people. It became one at a time, although that was still not God's way. Real healing for me began when I started paying more attention to myself and my daughter. It also was a time of focusing on my relationship with God or lack thereof.

The key to healing was being in the right place, with the right mindset, and the right people. DCC was a place of healing and where I received answers to my prayers. In my conversations with God, I would ask for answers, and God would provide the solutions through Bishop Nelson. That, in itself, helped me to know DCC was the place for me, but there was some hurt from people there as well. I know I live in a dream world, and I want everyone to be happy and to just love one another. When you have been through what I've been through, you want true, genuine love.

I started seeing a counselor. This took my healing process to another level. After about 15 weeks with one and five with another, I did not see a difference. I could talk all day, but some demons refused to let go. Still, I was clueless as to what they were. Yes, my counseling should have been longer, but it was not. I had a terrible habit of beginning things and quitting before I saw results. I also lacked the money to get the care I needed. There was always great intention on my behalf for me to be healed, but it was not my time yet.

I did what the counselors asked of me, and I was very true about whatever was asked. I enjoyed the sessions, but they came to a halt. I remember the last session, as I informed the counselor that I needed to take a break (due to my finances), and I never returned. I even searched for other counselors, but they referred me to someone else, so I gave up. The spirit of quitting was nothing new to me.

I had always wanted to return to school to receive a degree. So I did. It was a major triumph for me since I was on the brink of dropping out during my senior year of high school. What was pushing me to want to attend college? I intended to become a certified life coach because that was the closest thing to being a counselor. In returning to school, I began to realize how intelligent I was.

I did quite well and continued to do so. Strangely, the courses for the coaching program were canceled. I was disappointed. I went to my advisor and asked him what I could do since my classes were being canceled. He informed me that I could also work on getting my AA degree while completing the coaching program, which is what I am doing. I am growing to know who I really am. I am learning that I can do anything I put my mind to. I'm finding that I love being in school. I made Dean's list twice and have not earned anything less than a 3.4 GPA.

A major component that helped me to heal was changing my mindset. This was a necessity as I was so negative and toxic to myself and others. I had to change my thoughts and my words. In changing those things, I grew and became more aware of myself and the decisions I was making. Due to the abuse, I was jaded and angry. I had to find ways to kill the negative thoughts before they manifested into actions. One way I changed my thoughts was to make positive affirmations as well as speak over my mind. When I felt a bad thought coming, I had to rebuke it in Jesus' name. When you learn how powerful you are and how to use that power, your mind shifts and you are no longer afraid to face the enemy that lives within.

I began to speak healing, peace, and wholeness over my mind. Learning and speaking Holy Bible scriptures was also a major part of healing for me. I would say,

"Let this mind be in me which is also in Christ Jesus,"

"No weapon formed against me shall prosper for I am more than a conqueror," and

"God did not give me a spirit of fear, but of power, love and a sound mind."

Those three scriptures were on my lips several times daily.

The enemy attacked my mind so much that I thought I was bipolar. My problem was that when God would purge me, I would not fill that void correctly, which allowed me to have setback after setback. It was a long road to healing, but I had to make up in my mind that I wanted to be delivered and healed so I could walk in God's perfect will for my life.

The healing came when I began to speak life and not death to myself. Life and death are in the power of the tongue, so I had to change my language and push through it. It was not an easy task, but I persevered. Changes also came when I began to renounce the demons that were attached to my family. I saw things manifest because my mind, heart, and spirit were changing. I began to not just listen to the word and build a stronger relationship with God, but worship became a daily part of my life.

I was "Negative Nancy" and struggled to embrace the good things that happened to me. "I can't" was a major phrase in my vocabulary. If I made a mistake, I would beat myself up for days even though God had already forgiven me. I just did not know how to forgive myself and move forward. Ryan Roy, my life coach, was the person who helped with that.

He came in and held me accountable for everything. I was always busy but not productive. He helped me to see that I had so much potential and that I needed to harness it in the right direction. He also helped me to change the way I thought about myself. In hiring him as a coach, I was able to focus on the good I do each week instead of beating myself up so much. After a short time working with him, I have accomplished so much.

For me, anything outside of attending church that had to do with my spirituality was hard. It was hard for me to pray as well as read the Holy Bible. But when I learned about the demons, I understood it better. When there is a strong purpose on your life, the enemy fights you harder. Whenever I began to read the Holy Bible, I would instantly become tired. I would always start something full steam ahead, only to fizzle after a few months.

I began to ask myself, "How do I move forward and not allow the distractions to continue to hinder me? Why were these things so hard for me to do?" I wanted more of God, but how could I grow in Him if I could not even read His word or spend quality time with Him? I enjoyed Bible Study and attending other churches. I wanted to hear the word and allow it to penetrate my spirit. I wanted another level of God. Where I was spiritually seemed so elementary. It felt like I was in the toddler stage for most of my life.

I was tired of baby milk and wanted to inhale the fullness of God. I wanted a meal that would leave a savory, yet full taste in my spirit. I received that at DCC, but my flesh made me feel as if I did not. I continued to seek out ways to grow in God and found a wonderful app called "Periscope." Periscope is an app where you can watch live broadcasts and interact with whoever is giving the presentation. I came across men and women who spoke about deliverance, which was what I needed. I needed to know how to handle the demons and understand the attacks, so I began watching leaders who specialized in deliverance.

What I learned from watching them was that demons enter in all types of ways, but the demons had to be rebuked, cast out, and the permission between you and them had to be rescinded. I had to learn what my demons were before I could do anything, but I began to purchase books and read what I could. This also played a major part in my healing because as the demons were removed, I began to see things in a more positive light. I was able to release some things that I had been holding on to for years. Bishop Nelson also played an intricate role as many times he prayed over me, laid hands on me, and demons were released.

Whenever I needed to meet with him, it was scheduled. He never put his foot on my neck and made me feel worthless, but he counseled me in such a way that healing was imminent. We all need that father figure who speaks healing and nurtures us the best way they know how. I know this is going to sound nasty, but one way of release or my way of release is through vomiting. I would feel so bad because the altar workers had to clean it up, but I was being freed. In becoming free through the release, prayer, and consecration, I was able to break away from the spirits(demons) of lust, perversion, attention deficit, and low self-esteem, just to name a few.

I no longer wanted to watch porn, masturbate, or have casual sex. The freedom from the spirits also allowed me to completely abstain from sex. There had been plenty of times where I refrained, but this time the taste of abstinence was a huge victory for me. I no longer hungered or thirst for someone to be inside of me or touching me the way I had in the past. Back then, it was as if I would die if I did not have it.

Today, I have to be intentional about what I watch as well as what I listen to. Everyone knows that Jill Scott is my favorite artist and we know she talks about love and being intimate. But I now know what I can handle and when. If I am feeling aroused by music, I know that I have to turn away from it.

Through reading the Holy Bible and other books, prayer, fasting, hearing the word of God, positive affirmations, journaling and learning how to forgive has taken me to a level of healing that I never thought I would reach. I am no longer bitter, angry or wanting to take revenge on people. I am moving forward in what God has called me to do, and I am excited about it. I am not saying that I am completely healed because I still have a way to go, but I want every woman, man, boy, and girl to realize that they too can become free from their past. It truly takes hard work, consistency, dedication and a support team that will push you no matter how many times you feel like giving up. Being broken is not a horrible thing, but staying broken is.

Release everyone who does not add value to your life. No matter how long you have known them or how close you are to them, they are poison to you.

Surround yourself with a strong foundation of spirit-filled people who will love on you and cover you until you are capable of doing it for yourself and others. Run to God and allow Him to work His miracles in your life. I'm cheering for you because I know you have it in you.

Questions

There is a possibility that you may have or are living with unhealthy self-esteem. Answer the questions below to see where your level of self-esteem is.

List two ways that you can build your self-esteem?

_____

_____

_____

_____

Who or what makes you feel good about yourself?

_____

_____

_____

_____

Complete a list of what you would like to be healed from. Next, make a list of the things you think would help in the process.

_____

_____

_____

_____

You Got This!

When you change your mind, you change your life. The past happened, and there is nothing you can do about it but heal and move forward. Look at how it affected your life. Now, see your potential for growth and embrace it. You are more powerful and capable of overcoming every negative thing more than you know. Release the guilt, shame, and fear that you're holding on to. You have no need to be fearful, ashamed, or guilty. You are strong, creative, intelligent, beautiful, and brilliant. You are the apple of God's eyes. Now, change your perspective from victim to victor. Get out of the slump and stop allowing yourself to think you are undeserving of a great life. You can and will have every bit of freedom and happiness that awaits you. Arise lifesaver and take your place.

Chapter 7

What Has Come Over Me-The Demons Within

This chapter provides some of the groupings of the spirits (demons) I lived with that may be affecting you. It's a suggestive list of what you may encounter and this is in no way an exhaustive list. This only provides a small glimpse of the symptoms you may or may not encounter. Do not allow this to scare you, but I suggest that you reflect on some of your mannerisms, habits, feelings, and desires, which will make you aware of your emotions or why you may do some of the things you do. With sexual assault, you are or have been opened up to things that you had no business being opened up to. You must come out of agreement and be delivered from these spirits. As long as you are in agreement, they will hang around and torment you daily. If you are not spiritually or mentally strong enough or know what deliverance entails, seek out a pastor or ministry that walks in deliverance.

With the permission of Pastor Beverly Tucker, author of "Setting the Captives Free -Deliverance Manual," here are some of the groupings we fall prey to. The Root (stronghold) is listed first and then the spirits that are connected. This list does not provide every grouping, due to me not wanting to overwhelm you.

Sexual Abuse Grouping

Addiction, Alienation, Amnesia, Behavioral Change, Blocked Memories, Damaged Emotions, Depression, Emotional Pain, Extreme Instability of the Personality, False Guilt, Fear, Fear of Intimacy, Guilt, Helplessness, Hopelessness, Inappropriate Acts, Isolation, Loss of Boundaries, Low or No Self-Esteem, Negative Emotional Bonding, Overly Sensitive Emotions, Post-Sexual Abuse Trauma, Rage, Self-Centered, Self-Sabotage, Feeling Stupid, Suicidal Ideation, Suppression, Trauma, Traumatic Stress Syndrome, Triggers

Rape Victims Grouping

Anger, Anxiety, Confusion, Defiled, Degraded, Depression, Embarrassment, Fondling, Guilt, Hate, Humiliation, Succubus, Incubus, Obsessive Compulsive Disorder (OCD), Loss of Trust, Lust, Lust of the Eyes: Flesh, Pornography, Powerlessness, Promiscuity, Rage, Revenge,

Self-Hate, Sexual Molestation, Shame, Unclean, Unrestrained Passions, Unrestrained Lusts, Violated, Violence

Lust: adultery, fornication, masturbation, pornography, perversion, rape, and sexual impurity.

Pride: arrogance, haughtiness, self-righteousness, vanity, ego, and perfection.

Rejection: rejection from the womb, self-rejection, hurt, deep hurt, bitterness, anger, hatred, fear of rejection, fear, insecurity, depression, sadness, loneliness

Bitterness: resentment, hatred, unforgiveness, violence, temper, anger, retaliation, murder

Insecurity: Inferiority, self-pity, loneliness, timidity, shyness, inadequacy ineptness

Depression: despair, despondency, discouragement, defeatism, dejection, hopelessness, suicide, death, insomnia, morbidity

Perfection: pride, vanity, ego, frustration, criticism, irritability, intolerance, anger

Sexual Impurity: lust, fantasy lust, masturbation, homosexuality, lesbianism, adultery, fornication, incest, harlotry, rape, exposure, frigidity

Self-Accusation: Self-hatred, self-condemnation

Guilt – The definition of guilt is the state of one who has committed an offense, especially consciously. There is no reason why a survivor of sexual assault should have a feeling of guilt as there is nothing you could have done to offend or cause anyone to take anything from you. You were innocent. You were victimized.

Guilt will have you walking around thinking you did something, although you did not. You should never feel that being sexually assaulted or abused is your fault. Dealing with guilt can greatly affect your self-esteem. When you release the guilt that you are holding on to, it shows that you are on your way to truly loving yourself. Dealing with it allows you to begin to live a healthier life and allows more positive feelings to flow.

Shame – The definition of shame is a painful feeling of humiliation or distress caused by the consciousness of foolish behavior. Shame comes in when you allow someone to come in and cast disgrace on you for something that happened to you that may not have been your fault. It puts you in an embarrassing place. My shame came from being molested, but also from freely allowing others to do as they pleased to me. Shame makes you feel unacceptable, undesirable, dirty, and disgusting. There were plenty of days I would literally try to scrub my skin off, trying to make that feeling go away. A spirit of shame keeps you from healing or allowing anyone to help you because you think that 'thing' that happened to you is humiliating, and people will talk about you or hurt you further. If you have the spirit of shame on you, please remember that the Holy Bible reads in Romans 8:1,

"Therefore, there is no condemnation for those who are in Christ Jesus for the law of the spirit of life in Christ Jesus has set you free from the law of sin and death."

God loves you and forgives you, but the enemy condemns you.

Low Self-Esteem – This is a lack of one's own confidence in themselves. Low self-esteem makes you feel unworthy and unattractive (inside and out). Low self-esteem causes you to nitpick every little thing you do. It makes you feel as though you are never good enough for anyone or anything. You don't know the power of speaking well about yourself or speaking life unto yourself. You don't realize just how amazing you are. Low self-esteem can come from not being affirmed by your parents or guardians. It can be brought on by peers due to bullying or teasing. You feel inadequate because Sheila has long hair or the latest designer apparel, but you don't have those things, and everyone makes Sheila feel special because she does. Honey, your soul is way more important than that $6,000 handbag that even Sheila can't afford. When you learn how to speak highly of yourself and receive compliments, you are on your way to achieving healthy self-esteem.

Lust and Perversion – This refers to a strong or obsessive craving for someone or something. Perversion - any of various means of obtaining sexual gratification that is generally regarded as being abnormal. Lust and perversion are two spirits that come heavily attached to sexual assault/abuse. We often wonder why little girls are so promiscuous, but we hesitate to contemplate whether something happened to them to make them that way. Lust and perversion cause us to either explore our sexuality sooner or to become a recluse. Lust and perversion can draw other spirits that keep us bound. Lust and perversion will have you chasing after attention and affection from the wrong places. You will give of yourself so freely sexually, that if you don't become free, you are killing yourself inside. Just know that porn and masturbation are of the enemy as well. These two spirits will have you participating in sex with any and everyone, and you do not give a second thought to it. It may be several times a day, and you feel as though you never get enough. Sounds like an addiction, right? Well, it is. Your body is the temple of the Holy Spirit, and you must see and treat it as such. This takes much self-love and care.

Lack of intimacy – In regards to intimacy, the abused deal with multiple issues. Some shy away from sex and if they engage in intercourse, they lie there numb. Others believe that their worth is sexually based and that is how the measurement they use to value themselves. Others are confused and have a hard time conceiving whether they wish to engage in sex or not. One of the issues I face was being able to say no to sex that I did not wish to have, while other times, I could not get enough. Some survivors find pleasure in sadistic encounters or things dealing with fantasy. Not all abusers have issues with intercourse, but they are not able to build close relationships with others, whether sexual or not. I often felt if someone did not want to have sex with me, they did not love me.

Bitterness – (Of people or their feelings or behavior) anger, hurt, or resentfulness because of one's bad experiences or a sense of unjust treatment. Bitterness comes when you hold on to past hurts and pain. You must learn how to release things immediately, as bitterness can cause many illnesses that you may not even be aware of. Bitterness can enter when you have allowed yourself to trust and talk to someone about your abuse, but they do not believe you. I allowed bitterness in due to being abused in multiple manners. I held on to being angry, which turned into bitterness. If you have been harping on a situation, a circumstance or something that happened to you for years, there is a chance that you are bitter. No matter what takes place in your life, whether good or bad, you have that sour taste in your mouth. Yes, my dear, that is bitterness. Please let it go and allow God to heal and use you.

Rejection - "the act of not accepting, believing, or considering something: the state of being rejected." In a world of trauma, you don't have the opportunity to know who you really are easily. You look for love and acceptance from all aspects of life. It gives you a spirit of perfectionism, making you think that one day, everything you do will be done perfectly. Rejection will have you looking desperate without even realizing it. Rejection also causes you to sabotage relationships. You do what you feel is necessary to get out of the relationship before the other person hurts you. The problem is they have no intention of hurting you. Rejection allows you to seek out attention no matter how you get it. You do whatever it takes to befriend people even if you really don't want to do what they ask. You just want to feel loved and wanted. You are rejecting every good thing that can come into your life.

In Romans 8:31, the Bible tells us, "What, then, shall we say in response to these things? If God is for us, who can be against us? Know that God is for you. He loves you and wants nothing but the best for you. The Bible also relays to us that when our parents forsake us, God takes us up. From this point on, embrace a better understanding of how God sees you, protects you and takes care of you. People will come and go in your life, but God remains forever. He's such a gentleman that He won't force Himself on you, but if you seek Him with everything in you, He will be right there. You also have to do your part by falling in love with yourself.

Love on yourself and become accepting of everything you deserve. You have to get to know who you truly are—who God made you to be. Not who you want to be or people have told you that you are. Find verses in the Bible that tell you who you are in God and recite them daily. Celebrate your victories. Celebrate yourself. Treat yourself well. Take yourself out on dates. Speak healing, wholeness, and life over yourself. Change your language. Speak love, strength, beauty, and loving words to yourself. Here are a few scriptures to help you.

"I am beautiful." – Ecclesiastes 3:11

"I am courageous and strong." – 1 Chronicles 28:20

"I am inseparable from His love." – Romans 8:35

"I am the image of God." – Genesis 1:27

"I am holy and blameless." – Ephesians 1:4

"I am God's workmanship." – Ephesians 2:10

"I am given His divine power and promises." - 2 Peter 1:3-4

"I am every good thing." – Philemon 6

"I am created in Christ for good works." – Ephesians 2:10

"I am wonderfully and fearfully made." – Psalm 139:14

Fear - an unpleasant, often strong emotion caused by anticipation or awareness of danger. The real problem with fear is that we become fearful when we are not aware of what the outcome will be. Sometimes, we are just scared of succeeding. We struggle with being able to trust people, which keeps us from building successful relationships. I was fearful of being single for the rest of my life. I was fearful of not having friends. I was even fearful that there would be no one at my funeral when I die. In building relationships, we remain guarded because we believe that they will hurt us just like our abuser(s). Any type of noise, movement, scent or familiar place or event can trigger fear in us. Sometimes it is so bad that we don't come out of our homes. Fear is a trick of the enemy. As 2 Timothy 1:7 states,

"God did not give us a spirit of fear, but of power, love and a sound mind."

We must constantly remind ourselves of this scripture when we become fearful.

Unforgiveness – Not willing to give mercy to someone who hurt you. Unforgiveness can cause you illness and so much hurt. If you are unwilling to show mercy and not forgive, you can cause your heart to become hardened. Think about it. Jesus died for your sins so that you have new mercies daily, and He forgives you easily. Unforgiveness can turn into bitterness. Yes, it is very hard to forgive someone who sexually assaulted you.

Give some thought to Biblical figures who committed murders, were thieves, committed adultery and more. Still, God forgave them. Yes, they hurt you, but just as you receive new mercies, you should have it in your heart to offer mercy—to forgive and move forward with life. For years, it was hard for me to forgive myself and my abusers, but I was only doing more internal damage to myself. Forgiveness is a major part of the healing process. Healing also is more for the broken than the abuser. Don't miss out on a great life because you can't forgive.

Ephesians 4:31-32 is very clear on forgiveness.

"Get rid of all bitterness, rage and slander, brawling and slander, along with every form of malice. Be kind and compassionate to one another, forgiving each other, just as in Christ God forgave you."

I was able to tell Arturio that I forgave him, and it was a weight lifted off my shoulders. He apologized to me and informed me that God had dealt with him. I was able to talk to him about what he did to me as a child. It says that we shall reap what we sow. He shared with me that he was in a horrible accident that caused him to have brain surgery, his eye being placed back into the socket, and paralyzed due to being hit by two cars. As he prayed for God to take him from the earth, God asked him, "Where is your faith?" To me, that says God forgave him. Who was I not to forgive him? I pray that his relationship with God will continue to grow stronger as he is completely healed.

Sadly, some of you wish death upon your abusers. You are wishing Arturio's injuries worse for what he did. But those are not the right thoughts to have. Yes, sexually abusing a child is a sin and a terrible thing to do. But the God I serve is a forgiving God and is even able to forgive an abuser. God forgave me for all the foolishness I carried out and for being the rebellious child who was a hypocrite. Why not forgive someone if they mean it and have changed their ways?

I desire to help the abused as much as I can. So you are aware of how damaging sexual abuse is, not just to your physical, emotional and mental being, but also to your spiritual being. I have received permission from Pastor Bev Tucker, who is a deliverance minister, to share a part of her deliverance manual with you. The section is at the end and it entails the spirits that group together in those that have been sexually abused. You may not have them all, but I'm sure you will recognize those you do. If there is anything you have questions about, please don't hesitate to contact Pastor Bev. Her information is included. We all need deliverance.

Well, there you have it! Although it does not give a complete account of my life in its entirety, you have a better understanding of what I experienced—casual, unsafe sex, mental torment and anguish, not walking in God's calling for my life, suicidal tendencies and so much more. With the help of God, I am still here. I lived through months of therapy because of a nervous breakdown. But, I am still here. I went from bed to bed and partner to partner, but I'm still here. I survived without a close-knit family or many friends. I am still here.

I am not rich monetarily. But I am rich in spirit and the wisdom that comes from life lessons. I could have been selfish and not share my story, but I want you to be healed. I want you to come out from hiding because you are a needed entity in this world. I shared because I knew that you were waiting on me. I shared because, although I don't know you, I love you. I shared because I believe you, I believe in you, and I know you are a survivor. I know you needed to hear that you are not alone in this. I am here to listen to you, to hug you, and to cheer you on. Whatever you want to do in life, you still have time to do it. Guess what? You also have the resources, but you just don't know it. A healthy way of living is available to you, but you have to want it.

Through the abuse, anguish, rejection, torment of the mind and low self-esteem, I survived! If you are a survivor of any type of abuse, you know what I am speaking of. It was a rough road, but we're still here. With the loss of friends, family members, and those I thought loved me, I am still in my right mind. I am now functioning in a capacity that I never thought I would be able to. There is nothing in this world that you or I cannot do if we put our minds to it. What were your dreams as a child? What do you dream of doing now? I need you to know that you can do all of it.

Have you forgiven yourself? Have you forgiven your abuser? Have you begun to love yourself and allow the broken places to be healed? Are you still beating yourself up? Are you still feeling guilty and ashamed? Are you still blaming yourself for what happened, and it was not even close to being your fault? Well, not only do you need to work on it for yourself, but for those that are waiting on you.

You cannot provide healing until you have been healed. How often do you speak peace and love to yourself? How many times do you hug yourself or take yourself out on a date? Do you take yourself to the doctor for regular visits? I ask this series of questions because I want you to realize the things you do when you are not healed and truly love yourself. You must understand that there is nothing wrong with you! It's not your fault! I just can't say that enough.

When you remove yourself from toxic environments and people, you are allowing yourself time to heal. You are saying to yourself that you love you enough to be healed and live a healthy life. You are telling yourself that you deserve to live and enjoy life. Don't rush back into a relationship until you know who you are.

You must fall so deeply in love with yourself that you see foolishness coming before it gets close to you. Love yourself so much that you can walk away from any relationship that is not beneficial to you. You deserve the absolute best life has to offer.

You deserve to be happy, healthy and living a rich life. You must understand that you are precious and valuable to God. People are waiting on you. Yes, you. You are a necessary voice in this world, and you have the power to change lives. You are a superhero in your own right. You see, your cape remains hidden but always comes out at the right time. Think about the strangers who just walk up to you and begin telling you their story. Think about those who try to connect with you, and you are clueless as to why. They see the greatness within you and want to know how you got it. They NEED you!

I suggest that you begin to love on yourself so that others will begin to love you authentically. One way to start your healing and start your journey to self-love is to write letters of forgiveness. Believe it or not, you blame yourself more than you blame your abuser(s). Draft one to yourself and one to all of your abusers. If you do not wish to send it to them, you do not have to, but if you do, that would be a major accomplishment as well. They need to know how they made you feel and what you have been carrying around for years.

Pour out your feelings, be completely honest with how it made you feel, what you think about them, and how you managed to survive. You won't be able to do this until you honestly forgive them. You will know when you have forgiven them because when you see them or someone mentions their name, you don't flinch, you don't cry, there are no knots in your stomach, you don't frown, or leave the room. I hear you saying that you will never get to this point, but you will. I have been in the same room with my abuser, and I thought I was healed, but I wanted to hurt him. To be honest, I wanted to kill him.

I would also like to recommend that you attempt to do mirror work on a daily basis. Mirror work requires discipline and the willingness to change. Mirror work causes you to face yourself and eventually embrace yourself. There are various levels to mirror work, but I suggest that you begin with loving on yourself. My preference is that you stand in front of a mirror and speak love to yourself. Start with your hair and work your way down to your toes. Yes, I said your toes.

You must change how you feel and think about yourself in every aspect. From your inner self to your outer self, your family, your name, and everything else about you. For example, I use to hate my entire name, but as you read, I provide you with my full name. You can't know who you are without knowing what your name means. Research your name. Your name speaks as to who you are. In learning my name, it helped me to love myself and everything about me.

It is as simple as saying to yourself in the mirror, "I love my eyes." "I love my small, brown eyes." "I love how pure my heart is." "I love the name I was given because it identifies the greatness in me and who I am." If you are bold enough, do it in the nude. Most of us don't like the way we look in our birthday suit, but you must change that as well. It takes a lot of work to be healed, but you deserve to be free.

Another suggestion is to journal. If I had not done it for myself, I would not believe it. Journaling was such a major healing place for me. Every time I put pen or pencil to paper, another level of healing occurred. Journaling allows you to express your feelings, your thoughts, as well as provides a reminder of your growth down the road. Journaling will allow you to realize whether you have been healed or not. It will allow you to express yourself without being judged or having to talk about it. It will also allow you to go back and see how much you have grown over the years and the accomplishments you've made along the way.

After years of abuse—both self-imposed and imposed by others—I am healed, healthy and no longer suffer from "stinking thinking." When you change your mind, you change your life. Your thoughts play a major role in your daily process. When you overcome the negative thoughts and learn how to overcome negative self-talk, you can live a life so abundant that you will be mad at yourself for taking so long to do so. I know I did. I am acutely aware of my surroundings and who I allow in my space. I have never been more protective of myself since I came to a place of healing. I love myself, and I will never allow another person to physically, mentally, or emotionally hurt me again. I want you to be able to do the same thing.

The strong, authentic person in you needed to come forth so you can carry out the purpose in which you were created. If you dreamed it and can envision it, you can achieve it. Obtain the healing and discipline that is necessary to achieve your dreams.

Remain focused on what you desire to accomplish and fight through it. DO NOT allow anyone, including yourself, to talk you out of it. You have to know deep down in your heart that *you got this* and Heaven has your back. You don't have to be fearful, stressed, depressed, doubtful or feel incompetent. God has placed everything in you that you need to be successful.

You managed to survive abuse, addictions, suicide attempts, and so much more. Don't tell me you can't accomplish your dreams. It took a fight to survive through those things, and they affected you in a negative manner. Just think how much you can accomplish in a positive mindset, with an amazing support system and fighting the right way.

With everything I endured, I am now a retired model and actress, as well as a college graduate. I've raised a beautiful and intelligent daughter. I found the strength to speak openly to whomever will listen, including speaking at conferences. I've completed this book, won speaking contests, as well as having clients I coach. One day I will be counseling and may even get back into acting and singing and many other things that interest me. What is holding you back? I am no different than you.

A dream does not have to remain a dream; it can become a reality. My dreams included being an opera singer, a model, a stuntwoman, and an actress. I don't think two out of four is bad. I have been published as a model, walked over a hundred catwalks, sang in several studios on my projects and those of others. No, I'm not bragging. But I want to help you understand that your best life is awaiting you. The abuse or issues you have survived DOES NOT define who you are. You survived your tragic circumstances so that your faith, strength, and character could be heightened. It helped you build up the characteristics that you needed to develop so you could be the authentic, powerful person you were meant to be.

Hold your head up high, throw your shoulders back, and be the beautiful, bold, gifted, creative person you were meant to be. Chase those dreams. There are abundant resources to assist you. Family and friends may want to help you as well. Use every gift and talent that God provided you. If you don't know what they are, reflect on the things you love to do.

Think about the things you would do for the rest of your life, even if you weren't being paid to do them. Your supporters, your clients, your friends, your armor-bearers, and angels are waiting on you. When you leave this earth, leave empty. What I mean is that you should pursue everything you have ever wanted to do without ever looking back. Every gift and talent that you were given—use them!

Imagine yourself living the lifestyle you desire, being filled with joy, peace and an abundance of love. Imagine your name in lights or rolling in movie credits, being supermom, your face on a television or movie screen, or maybe your book being an #1 international bestseller for decades. How about becoming the attorney, doctor, or musician you wanted to become? No matter the age, you are not too old to pursue it.

Can you imagine you achieving those things?

I can!

Warning Signs of Possible Abuse to Your Children

As much as we would like to be with our babies 24/7, we cannot always do so. Here are just a few signs to look for if you think your child(ren) have been abused. One thing I do advise is DON'T KEEP SECRETS! Have conversations with your child(ren) and let them know that they can talk to you about anything. If you establish an open relationship with them, you won't have to worry about them keeping things from you. If any of these things have happened or are happening, it could be due to something else as well. This is not a complete list, but I wanted to provide a few signs.

1. Inquire (Investigate) about the people your child(ren) will be around. People keep secrets and you may not always see who lives in the dwelling where your child frequents. If that child(ren) adamantly informs you that they no longer wish to go to or stay at that person's

home, don't make them go. There has to be a reason they no longer want to go. Comfort them and ask them why.

2. Do NOT name your children's private parts something other than what it is. If an adult asks your child(ren) if they can have some of their cookie, but the adult inappropriately touches your child(ren), you have to blame yourself. The child(ren) will tell them yes or question it because they may not be eating a cookie. Abusers have clever ways of gaining trust and tricking their prey. Remember, children are little humans. Teach them the anatomically correct name of their body parts and you will know when someone has done something they had no business doing.

3. The child(ren) may be above the age of bedwetting or soiling, but still have that issue. Again, establishing a trusting relationship with your child will provide an everlasting opportunity for them to tell you any and everything.

4. They will begin to talk about sex or try to perform sexual acts. They may try to touch your private area or you may see them trying to do sexual things with other children.

5. They may begin to have headaches and chronic stomach pain. Schedule an appointment for them to see their physician.

6. Their attitude towards family, friends, things they enjoy, and school may change to anger and increased signs of aggression.

7. Rebellion and isolation may occur, along with self-mutilation.

8. A change in appetite.

9. Fear and anxiety may set in.

10. Sleeping patterns change. Possible nightmares take place.

Chapter 8

Welcome to the Healing Place

T he first thing you must do is to admit that you were abused. This is a very important step. Admit is defined as: to concede as true or valid; to acknowledge or assent to, as an allegation which it is impossible to deny; to own or confess. Anything we deal with in life, whether good or bad, must be faced head-on. It happened. You must admit and accept that. I know it will be hard, but you have to be brave enough to talk about it so you can begin to heal. You can write it out, speak about it, or find someone you can confide in. Admitting it is the truth and the beginning of a beautiful life. Until you admit it, you will remain in the dark and continue to lie to yourself. You deserve the truth in every aspect.

Upon admitting it, you must then, accept it. Yes, I know you think I'm crazy and I need to see a therapist. Well, I'm still seeing one. Most of us don't want to admit it, let alone, accept it. Again, you must be honest with yourself and realize it's not who you are but an ordeal you survived through. Accept means to receive with favor, to approve, to understand Jesus is the first person that comes to mind when it comes to accepting something. Consider when He went to the Garden of Gethsemane and asked God, "Let this cup pass from me." Yes, God was Jesus in human form, which allowed Him to feel the things we feel, but in the end, He did accept it, which is why we are here. Another example is Job. Job lost everything and even with his wife being infuriated and telling him to just curse God and die, Job continued to bless God throughout His trials, accepted what was taking place and at the end, received double for all that he lost. I know we wish it wasn't true or it didn't happen, but healing is a process of honesty.

Thirdly, you must announce to someone that it happened. Announced is defined as: to give public notice, or first notice of; to make known; to publish, to proclaim. Every secret that you're holding on to, you're dwelling in darkness. 1st John1:9 says, "If we confess our sins, He is faithful and just to forgive us our sins and to cleanse us from all unrighteousness." Before you begin yelling that you did not commit a sin, a sin took place. You were abused and from that, if you were not immediately delivered, you committed other sins. Whether you became addicted to sex, pornography, drugs, cutting, homosexuality or lesbianism, it's a sin. "This then is the message which we have heard of him, and declare unto you that God is light and in Him is no darkness at all." Again, every secret is darkness. We know that dark and light cannot dwell together. Whatever secrets we contain, the enemy is snickering at us and saying, "Gotem!" They are too ashamed, fearful and guilt-ridden to say anything so let's see how much longer I can keep my foot on their neck, oppressed, depressed, suicidal and broken. God clearly tells us that "Whom the Son sets free is truly free indeed." You have to desire freedom instead of bitterness, pain and torture.

Next, find a therapist. This is "a must" in the process. A therapist can assist you in sorting out what happened, as well as getting you to express your feelings. You may also be suppressing what happened or how it makes you feel. It is important that you work your way through this. Please remember that this is a process and it will take time.

While going through therapy, you will need a support system in place. A support system may consist of family members, friends, a support group, or peers who will be there when you need emotional support. They can provide a listening ear or supply a trusting relationship that takes you out of isolation. A support system can provide the loving environment you will need due to the vulnerability and transparency that will take place during your therapy sessions. Your support system must include those you trust — people you know will be there when you need them most. One of the most important things is that you must trust yourself as well. You must believe in yourself and set boundaries so that no one will ever walk over you or do the things that were done to you that will produce a broken state ever again.

Several journals or notebooks will be needed as well. For some, putting pen to paper is a type of therapy all on its own. I suggest that you write what you discuss in the counseling session. Write down your feelings, things that you think about, and things you wish to change. During your time of healing, it is very important to write. First, it helps to reflect on your growth and what happened to you. It also provides you with documentation of your success as you heal. It gives you a way of tracking your progress. You can keep assignments from your therapist there as well.

Therapy sessions will be intense and will take you through a myriad of emotions and doubt. In the process, you will find out who you are. You must have balance in your life. I suggest you find hobbies—activities that you enjoy participating in. Whether it's reading, crocheting, attending the opera or ballet, cooking, sewing, traveling, dining out, or hiking, begin to do more of those things if you aren't already. Things that make you happy or are exciting to you will simultaneously invigorate you and relax you.

Finding hobbies and discovering your likes and dislikes will also assist in you getting to know who you are and what you like beyond the pain. As victims of sexual assault and domestic violence, we tend to believe that the trauma *is* us. We fail to understand that it was something that happened *to* us. You are entitled to a great life, and this is a part of finding out what you want in your life.

I cannot tell you when you will be able to forgive yourself and your abuser, but you will know when it's time; that is also a very important step in healing. Forgive yourself for the mental and emotional abuse you put yourself through. Forgive your abuser for what they have done to you as well. When you truly forgive yourself and your abuser, you no longer allow the trauma to be held over your head. You no longer flinch when you see them or when something reminds you of them. You may overcome the ability to be mentally, emotionally, and physically triggered by memories of them.

Sometimes, when we go through traumatic ordeals, we shut down any physical involvement. There are some of us who actually go the opposite direction and are overly sexual. You must forgive so you can pursue and continue to have a normal life. Forgiveness is more for you than your abuser. If you are unable to forgive, you're holding yourself hostage; the abuser has moved on with his or her life. Forgiveness will free your heart of anger, bitterness and other negative emotions you may be clinging to.

Finally, breathe. Embrace this process and what you endured. The fact of the matter is you are still here. Stop merely existing, and begin to thrive in life. You have purpose; someone is waiting on you to help them walk through their journey. You were built for this. You have the strength for this. Make peace with yourself, your abuser, and your past. There are some tremendous things waiting ahead for you.

How would you respond to an apology from your abuser?

_____

_____

_____

_____

"Forgive as God forgave you." Colossians 3:13

Below, you will find an example of a letter of forgiveness to myself, as well as an abuser. Please write one to aid you in the process of forgiving yourself. Also, remember to write one to your abuser and anyone that has ever hurt you in life. Again, as I stated before, if you are brave enough, send it to them. If not, write the letter and shred it. The point is to write the letter. In your letter, include your emotions, how it made you feel, what it made you feel like to be in their presence, the daily turmoil and heartache you endured. You must be completely honest with yourself and with your abuser. Below you will find an example of a letter. The letter below is a letter of forgiveness I wrote to myself.

Forgiveness letter to self.

Dear Retta,

First, I want you to know that I love you very much. I know that you have endured a lot, but none of it was your fault. There were many who hurt you and used you. Although you have dealt with much, you are a strong woman. Secondly, I forgive you. Retta, I forgive you for the mental and emotional abuse, as well as the physical abuse.

I want you to take a deep look within yourself and truly release all the guilt, pain, and shame that you have endured. Let it go! You have suffered long enough and it's making you mean, bitter and hostile. It's okay to release it because God has something better. He loves you and wants better for you. I forgive you for all the beds you put me in and all the men you allowed in and out of me. I know you were in a broken place, but now it's time to be free. It's time to be delivered and live the life God intended for you.

Retta, I forgive you for not knowing who you are. By forgiving yourself, now you can move forward and begin to see how God loves you and take the time to love yourself. God sees you in such a different way than you see yourself. It's okay to cry because, in your tears, God cleanses you. You are beautiful, intelligent, funny, loving, transparent and vulnerable, loyal and caring to all.

Although they told you that you would never amount to anything or only be good for laying on your back, God has more for you. Things happened, but I forgive you and hope that you are now ready to forgive. It's been over two decades. Embrace who God has made you to be, a priest, His royal priesthood and daughter. You are an heir to His throne. He wants to dance with and converse with you. He wants you to sing praises to Him with the beautiful voice He has given you.

Retta, I wholeheartedly forgive you and I love you. It was not your fault and I look forward to living in peace, prosperity and all that God has for you. Let the healing begin. You deserve it. Here's to a great life.

Sincerely,

Me

Forgiveness letter to your abuser

Dear Jason,

This is Retta. I'm not sure if you remember me or not. I played with your son, Marcus, almost every day after school. It has been almost twenty-seven years since we have seen each other. I know it may be strange hearing from me, but I needed to contact you.

My life has been one of agony, emotional and mental turmoil. I will never forget what you did to me. You don't know how your actions affected my life. You took the innocence of a vulnerable child. What did I do to you to make you do that? I trusted you, as did my family. Was I the only one, were there others, I always wondered. You caused me to be angry, bitter, and emotionally unsound. I hated the world, myself and you.

I dealt with emotional turmoil daily, which kept me from realizing what true love is, due to your manipulation, because I could no longer trust anyone, including myself. You abused your power and it tore me to pieces. You caused me to have an identity crisis that I am still trying to survive through. With years of struggling with identity issues, low self-esteem, and other issues,

Guess what...

I forgive you. That's right. I forgive you for the hell you put me through. I pray that you have forgiven yourself and ask God to forgive you. I pray that your life is filled with peace, joy and the love of Almighty God. Please know that I am doing well and walking through the life that God intended for me. What the enemy meant for evil, God used it for my good and His glory.

Peace and Blessings to you always,

Retta

Imagine Me

Imagine me.....

No confidence, low self-esteem and ugly to boot

Imagine me....

Raped/molested, a private dancer, a prostitute

Imagine me....

A heart filled with hate, no self-love, anger and rage

I still try to figure out how I managed most days

Multiple sex partners, male and female, my inclination raised

Was it my hormones or maybe hunger, I suppose

Innocence taken at such an early age, unclean, un-pure and filled with lust and shame

Why take something that does not belong to you, to kill a precious child inside for your ungodly pleasure

Is that really how you are supposed to love or cherish a treasure

Suicide attempts, drunkenness, and all-out casual sex

Who is this person and why does she lack respect

Speak up and speak out from all your brokenness and hurt

Why is she here, what is her purpose, she is nasty and unclean

God's grace and mercy kept her safe, AIDS, death and even HIV

Because of God's perfect will and plan for her life, she still survives

He made her and loves her to no end.

Now, Imagine me….

Wonderfully, fearfully made, happy, delivered and set free, beautiful, intelligent, God-fearing and saved

Now, imagine you….At peace, full of purpose and loved, because you are a beautiful creation by God Almighty

www.ingramcontent.com/pod-product-compliance
Lightning Source LLC
Chambersburg PA
CBHW070800100426
42742CB00012B/2199